ONE
GOOD
QUESTION

HOW COUNTRIES
PREPARE YOUTH TO LEAD

RHONDA BROUSSARD

TBR Books
New York - Paris

TBR Books is a program of the Center for the Advancement of Languages, Education, and Communities. We publish researchers and practitioners who seek to engage diverse communities on topics related to education, languages, cultural history, and social initiatives.

CALEC - TBR Books

750 Lexington Avenue, 9th floor, New York, NY 10022, USA.

www.calec.org | contact@calec.org

Front Cover Design and Illustration: Ben D´Nagy, CARTEL

ISBN 9781636070841

Library of Congress Control Number: 2021950330

ONE
GOOD
QUESTION

HOW COUNTRIES
PREPARE YOUTH TO LEAD

RHONDA BROUSSARD

« FOR THESE ARE ALL OUR CHILDREN, WE WILL ALL PROFIT BY
OR PAY FOR WHAT THEY BECOME.»

-James Baldwin

ADVANCE PRAISE

"Posing good questions is essential to a meaningful life. Now is a good time for wondering — and working with others. This book demonstrates the richness of thinking together... and turning more ideas into actions. I just want to rush out and begin."

Bernardine Vester, Founder, Education Plus Auckland

"Visionary leaders approach knowledge with sharing, and often that sharing comes in the form of asking direct, simple, hard questions. One Good Question leads with this principle, and Rhonda's leadership and voice is the guide we need for these times and conversations."

Tre Johnson, author of *Black Genius*

"*One Good Question* engages readers in a deep reflective trajectory by interacting with probing questions that lead readers to their own 'one good question,' reconnecting them with their core beliefs about inclusive and quality education for all students. Thank you, Rhonda, for guiding my own self-reflection so masterfully!"

Ofelia G. Wade, Utah Spanish Dual Language Immersion Director

"As Clayton Christensen often said, questions create spaces in the brain for solutions to fall into. In this delightful read, Rhonda Broussard pushes us all to ask and answer the right questions — not the convenient ones — to help society make progress."

Michael B. Horn, author and cofounder of the Clayton Christensen Institute

"Whereas monolingualism is the illiteracy of the 21st century, equity is the foundation of the 21st century. Rhonda Broussard uniquely understands both and her book masterfully weaves key concepts of sustainable development in education by asking experts what their One Good Question is for a fair-minded education system of tomorrow!"

Gregg Roberts, Director, Dual Language Studies, American Councils Research Center

"In *One Good Question*, Rhonda Broussard models the essence of learning — curiosity. In following her genuine interest in discovering what will make for an equitable education system, Rhonda invites the reader into rich dialogue with some of the great thinkers and doers who are truly making it happen for kids every day, and in the process creates a map for anyone who cares about educating our youth."

Diane Tavenner, author of *Prepared: What Kids Need for a Full Life*

"Inspirational and informative. Broussard takes the timely questions we should all be asking, and brings us on a truly enjoyable journey to understand what kids and our schools need to lead in the future."

Stephanie Malia Krauss, author of *Making It: What Today's Kids*
Need for Tomorrow's World

"People who are serious about educating future generations as Rhonda Broussard is tend to possess a deep humility, an understanding that they must approach the task of education with more questions than answers and a joyful commitment to go where their curiosity and the resulting evidence lead them. This is not a book to read if you want your biases confirmed; it's a book to read if you are serious about putting your assumptions to the test. Broussard asks her 'one good question' to education leaders the whole world over. If you're committed to assisting the next generation in becoming global citizens, do yourself a favor and ponder their answers — and also their questions."

Jarvis DeBerry, author of *I Feel to Believe*

"How does one convince an entire culture that it has been asking the wrong questions? Further, that the act of learning to question might be an answer itself? In this smart and urgent collection, global educator Rhonda Broussard asks us to consider the revolutionary potential of a problem-posing approach to education in an era marked by widening social inequity, viral social media, and critical social justice. These visionary questions push us to imagine how different our worlds might look if we dared to possess the courage to approach the classroom (among other spaces) with less certainty and more wonderment, fewer fears of losing a foothold within capitalism and greater conviction in young peoples' capacity to lead us in reimagining. Relevant and well-researched, playful and provocative, this book paves the way for a dialogue about education that finally raises the stakes. And the questions."

Adam Falkner, author of *The Willies*

"In this book, *'One Good Question'*, Rhonda Broussard invites us to engage in conversation with a diverse group of voices who have each contributed their questions about the future, education, and our efforts to prepare the next generation to build a better future. Rhonda's introduction and conclusion, the multiplicity of perspectives included in the book, and the underlying structure of the book in bringing them together, makes for a refreshing invitation to think anew about what it means to educate global citizens."

Fernando M. Reimers, Ford Foundation Professor of International Education
Harvard Graduate School of Education

FOREWORD
BY KAYA HENDERSON

don't think that Rhonda — like so many women, and particularly many women of color — gives herself enough credit for the brilliance of her own ideas. Before I give Rhonda a chance to introduce her book, I want to sit with you to talk about the power of asking specific, probing, and meaningful questions. I'm not sure I realized it until I read her book, but the power that Rhonda finds in great questions is the same power that I have tapped into throughout my career in education. It has been the motivating force behind much of what I have accomplished as a teacher, as a district leader, and now as the founder and CEO of *Reconstruction*, an unapologetically Black education company.

I have innumerable examples of how big questions have helped me guide organizations to innovative solutions. I'll share a few of those with you shortly. Before I do that, however, I want to be clear about why the *One Good Question* way of thinking is so powerful and unique.

Most people look at education issues as tradeoffs. They speak in terms of zero-sum games and opportunity cost. They think of staffing tradeoffs, budget tradeoffs and policy tradeoffs. This approach can be appealing to the amateur economist in each of us, but it eliminates the opportunity to come up with creative solutions.

The downside of the "education as a series of tradeoffs" approach becomes clearer when we hear arguments that pit traditional public schools against charter schools, or when we make arguments to help us choose between closing two schools. "Education as a series of tradeoffs" has a destructive power which was made clearer, especially during the COVID-19 crisis, as opposing interest groups strove to win arguments for reopening schools or for staying virtual. We were scoring little wins and losses in the battle for authority over the schools while failing to ask good questions about what we can learn, how we can reshape school, and what approaches can benefit all of us. We were focused on tradeoffs and were not bothered to ask any good questions.

To be clear, I am not arguing for compromise, splitting the baby, or halfway solutions. Compromise, though necessary sometimes, is just another way of looking at education as a series of tradeoffs. It is an approach that forestalls victory for either side; it is as likely to delay a battle as it is to resolve one. Compromise may be an enlightened approach to resolving tradeoffs, but it is not an enlightened approach to improving education.

I served as the chancellor for DC Public Schools for six years, from 2010 through 2016. During this period, we were blessed with favorable conditions to improve education for our students. The population of the city as a whole was growing. We had a healthy economy. We had a sustainable governance structure and mayors who supported innovation in education. We were able to build on the challenging and disruptive work that came before us, and we fixed some of the most entrenched failures of the school district. We had the great opportunity that helped us think differently about education in our city.

It took Rhonda's book to help me realize the extent to which we had built our approach to education around that of *One Good Question*. Our question? How do we build a school system that provides what every parent wants for their own children? We often circled back to this question in our leadership team meetings.

Some answers came quickly and easily. We wanted great teachers. We wanted schools filled with joy. We wanted opportunities for students to learn a language, play a sport, and engage with music. We wanted all high school students to have the chance to take the most challenging classes and to match with colleges that will support their continued education.

Other answers emerged more slowly. I felt strongly that all students should have the chance to travel the world. Most of the parents on my leadership team had taken their own children abroad at some point, and as a traveler myself I knew how much international experiences can expand a child's worldview and can grow a child's confidence. I insisted that all our students had the opportunity to travel abroad twice — once in eighth grade and once in eleventh grade. Through the incredible work of our teaching and learning team, we helped hundreds of students get their first passports — and in some cases the luggage they needed — in order to travel to countries including China and Costa Rica.

The *One Good Question* approach is a power for policymakers to ask the right questions. When used, policymakers can come up with amazing ideas that do not fall into the tradeoff paradigm. We were able to offer international travel opportunities to all students with the use of funding, so the opportunity did not come at an expense. It wasn't a battle. It wasn't a compromise. We asked a good question — How do we build a school system that provides what every parent wants for their own children? — and got a great result.

The other hidden power of the *One Good Question* approach is that it invites people to join the conversation. While our question was a recurring theme in our leadership meetings, it also resonated in conversations with principals, teachers, and with parents. When you have a really good question, you want to hear as many answers as possible, and people who help you answer your question quickly become allies and thought partners rather than combatants. Asking a good question opens up opportunities for real involvement.

We applied this approach over and over again. We didn't ask which schools to close, we asked parents what services they wanted their children to enjoy at their neighborhood schools. We asked teachers what their very best lessons were, and we shared them with the whole district. We asked principals and school communities if they would like to expand learning time for students, and we asked how they would like to do so. In every case, great questions led to great ideas and to a broader coalition who wanted to ask the same questions.

Good questions continue to drive my work. *Reconstruction*, my most recent passion is an online tutoring program that expands the learning opportunities and interests of Black students. It started with one good question: How can we harness the knowledge and expertise of Black educators to provide amazing opportunities for Black students?

I am excited for Rhonda's book because I am excited for more educators and policymakers to recognize the amazing power of asking good questions. There was a time when we looked to education to bind us together. Perhaps that was too simple or naïve. We certainly have not seen education as a unifying force recently. Perhaps the thing that can bind us together is the good questions we are all driven to ask.

INTRODUCTION

'␣ve written this introduction ten different times. Writing a book in 2020 meant that I had to address 2020. The longer my writing stalled, the more 2020 demanded. There was the COVID-19 introduction. Then the George Floyd introduction. Then the post-George Floyd introduction. Then the executive-order-banning-critical-race-theory-in-professional-services introduction. Then the US presidential election where the-whole-world-is-watching us introduction. Then the post-election, pre-inauguration introduction. Then the insurrection introduction. Then the COVID-19 vaccine and variant strain introduction. When I reached the Amanda Gorman, *The Hill We Climb*, introduction, I was able to release some of the pain, frustration, and anxiety of the previous year. This book was quickly turning into a memoir of 2020 and reading Gorman's inauguration poem was what gave me the space to pause and decide what this book was really going to be about.

In 2015, I started a blog called "One Good Question," which was a series of interviews with global leaders and fellow inquirers. In the introduction to the blog, I shared my history of interrogation:

My premise? "I want to ask one good question."

That's all? I can ask one good question now. That's what I thought when I heard my colleague share her intellectual goal for the new school year. I had no idea how difficult it would be to ask my students one good question — a question that wasn't leading, that didn't tip my hand or reveal my beliefs, that didn't force students to defend a single position, nor one that did not allow them to respond solely with anecdotes and opinions.

In the fall of 2003, I was working with new peers in the second year of Baccalaureate School for Global Education in Queens, NY. This was the year that would challenge my teaching forever. Over ten years later, I'm still challenging myself to ask one good question. My work in international education has changed, but the need for good questions remains. In this blog I will be exploring international education and access for all students through multiple lenses, but all with the same question: In what ways do our investments in education reveal our beliefs about the next generation's role in the world?

Spoiler alert: I am completely biased. My education career is built on ways that are increasing access and opportunity for all students to connect with the world outside of their local neighborhood: multilingualism, cross-cultural and intercultural competencies, international perspectives, peacebuilding, youth action and agency, socio-economic diversity. I look forward to having my assumptions challenged and learning innovative ways that different countries, communities, and schools are answering this question.

What prepared me to write *One Good Question?*

I am a professional inquirer. In third grade our teacher called us *Wonder Whys*, which was great validation. I hope to never be too big or stubborn, or too certain, to ask questions.

My wonderings about education and equity led me to early action and commitment to student agency, particularly in urban communities. I was a teenage staffer at Summerbridge (now Breakthrough Collaborative) in New Orleans, LA, and Kansas City, MO, and interned at the national office in San Francisco, CA. I taught secondary students all over the country: high school in Ferguson, MO; drop-out recovery in Long Beach, CA; affluent suburban high school in Connecticut; and small secondary schools in Brooklyn and Queens.

I still believe that when educators make decisions as though all children are their children, they create more engaging, supportive, and challenging learning environments for everyone. My cross-country life as a French teacher led me to National Board Certification. And I thought I would stay in the classroom forever, but once I became a mother, my children inspired my foray into education entrepreneurship. In 2007, I founded and led an intentionally diverse network of public schools in St. Louis with language immersion and International Baccalaureate programs for all students. My education entrepreneurship led me to the Pahara-Aspen Fellowship, but when Michael Brown, Jr. was killed in Ferguson in 2014, my outlook on education changed. Our St. Louis community was at the center of national discourse on police violence and *#blacklivesmatter*. I was overwhelmed with the realization that I couldn't keep my own son safe, and that no diploma could stop a bullet. It did not matter what high school he went to or from which college he graduated; education alone will never be enough to humanize him for people who are committed to his demise.

That same fall my Eisenhower Fellowship afforded me the space to question my own work. I headed to New Zealand because their National Ministry of Education defines teaching as an inquiry. I wanted to spend time observing teaching as inquiry across grade levels and, hopefully, to learn to lead from a place of inquiry. When I returned to St. Louis, I didn't have any answers, I had something better: an awareness. I was consumed by the realization that in our school network, we were trying to get adults who had not learned via inquiry to teach through inquiry. Our professional development model was pretty unidirectional, so I started to wonder:

- How do you make space for adults to ask hard questions?
- How do you make space for educators to ask questions that encourage a change in their teaching practices?
- How do those educators then ask young people questions that lead to their own authentic learning and not just the "right" answer?

Ultimately, that was the space that I wanted to create with the *One Good Question* interview series.

What emerged?

Before I fully birthed the blog series, I started asking in 2015 what I thought was a bold, reflective question for the year. On my first morning in Havana for my friends' tenth wedding anniversary, we started the day with a guided tour of Old Havana. We were introduced to the tree *La Ceiba del Templete* and we learned about her place in Cuban history: she symbolized meetings, prayers, dreams, wishes, and gratitude. I took a solemn walk around La Ceiba three times, asking for clarity for the year ahead. My professional and love lives were exploding in ways that felt beyond me, and I hoped that La Ceiba would help me quiet my heart and brain, and eventually show me the right paths to solving dilemmas in both aspects of my life.

My ask for clarity was steeped in living life better — to work better, love better, improve outcomes, and change behaviors. I thought that getting clarity about my pain points at work and in my relationship would be the "right answers" and that La Ceiba would help me figure out how to execute them. As 2015 drew to a close, I had certainly gotten the clarity that I asked for, but the answers were not what I wanted. That December I was nursing a broken heart, in a painful work transition, and questioning everything once again. For 2016, however, I wanted to commit to asking the right questions, not necessarily getting the right answers. Something manageable between "What is the meaning of life?" and "What are my interim goal metrics?"

Around that time, Ravi Gupta penned an article about the need for students to engage in deep questioning, "When a student does not have courage, time, and space, their questions are often basic or vague — and sometimes don't even end with a question mark. 'Can you help me?' . . . 'I don't understand' . . . 'This is hard.'[1]" Sounds familiar? He had described my ask for clarity perfectly. I hadn't asked a deep question at La Ceiba, but instead just made a vague plea for help. What if I had applied his advice on questioning to guide my own adult inquiry?

There is a gap between what we ask for and what we actually need to learn. In Ian Leslie's book, *Curious: The Desire to Know and Why Your Future Depends on It*, he focuses on the paradox necessary to remain curious — understanding something enough to find it interesting, but having answers should not be too

---

[1] Gupta, Ravi "Teach Students to Ask More Questions" Education Reform, Medium. December 27, 2015. https://medium.com/education-reform/the-art-of-questioning-4617f3cd4a82

complex that questioning becomes overwhelming. The right question fits in that uncomfortable space, inspiring us to ask and giving us hope that the answer(s) are within reach.

In the months following that trip to Cuba, I started asking myself questions about my beliefs in education, wondering how I wanted to serve in the next phase of my career. Those questions were a step up from vagueness, but they were still statements in disguise. They were really easy to answer and justify with rich examples from my work. I had brilliant responses to those questions because they didn't force me to reconsider my position, to adopt a different perspective, or to incorporate what I had learned. Then it occurred to me that I couldn't answer my own questions with the same knowledge that asked it.

So, I went back to my inquiry and, this time, decided to ask my peers and colleagues around the world to weigh in. Not just the peers who would mirror my perspectives, but those who had completely different ways of seeing the question. In *One Good Question*, I ask international thought leaders and doers in education to reflect deeply on their country's investments, policies, and practices. Every interviewee noted that facing my one good question challenged their own thinking (victory for questioning!). For many, they were unsure if their country's leadership was asking themselves these types of essential questions to inform education design and reform. How many of their country's policies, state priorities, and school practices are based on the answers to the wrong questions?

There's an inherent tension in the urgency of public education transformation. I get it.

We don't feel like we have the luxury of time to reflect, iterate, and deepen adult learning because we're trying to make swift, scalable transformations for all kids. But if, as leaders — and by leader, I mean all of the ways that we lead in this movement — we're asking the wrong questions, those "wrong" questions will still give us answers.

How the chapters are organized

One Good Question is about making sustainable changes in education by centering the importance of questioning as a methodology. Ultimately, this book asks each of us to reflect on the biases in our current questions and theories. Whether you are a student, parent, teacher, administrator, advocate, minister or secretary of education, this book is an opportunity to create awareness about your own questions.

In the original interviews, I asked each leader three primary questions:

1. My one good question: "In what ways do our investments in education reveal our beliefs about the next generation's role in the world?" (To my surprise, no two leaders answered this the same way!)

2. The second question was always customized to their recent work — something that I was intensely curious about. For example: How do you get people to shift their values towards "education" not credential?

3. To close each interview I asked, "What's your one good question now? What are you wondering about?" I didn't expect their answer to relate to their current job or the content in our first two lines of inquiry.

Of course, each conversation included more than three questions, but this was the basic structure that we followed. Sometimes we recorded the conversations, but mostly I just typed away as we talked. I never knew where my questions would take us, so I was genuinely intrigued as each talk unfolded. Every interviewee had a final read of their piece before I published it in chronological order in the original blog. However, in this book I've taken a different approach. When I reread the original interviews — both published and unpublished — a few themes emerged:

1. **Education 2030, where are we headed?** Every international leader that I interviewed referenced the United Nations' Sustainable Development Goals (SDGs), and their specific expectations for education in 2030. The interviews in this chapter ground us in the goals.

2. **Are you preparing your students to become your peers?** In and out of school, are educators making space for youth to lead? The leaders in this chapter approach my question and their work from a youth development perspective.

3. **Who is following the money?** Even though my one good question names investment as a key tenet, not every leader directly addressed funding priorities. In this chapter we hear from leaders with more explicit economic and education funding perspectives.

4. **Who is benefitting from school redesign efforts?** Everyone sets out to redesign schools — to break from the industrial model — but who gets to attend redesigned schools? In this chapter we hear different perspectives on school redesign, including schools whose new design was immediately tested by COVID-19.

5. **What's language got to do with it?** How do schools engage our immigrant and multilingual students? To what extent are these programs serving their intended audience (students)? In this chapter we hear from linguists, biliteracy experts, neuroscientists, and advocates on the role of multilingualism in education.

6. **Who still needs to go to college?** (College or nah?) There have always been debates about whether or not college is for everyone. In this chapter education leaders explore what post-secondary attainment means for career paths.

7. **Do students have the right to agency in their own education?** So many educators that I spoke with stated that students should have more say in their education decision-making. From local building examples to policy examples, leaders in this chapter wonder in which ways administrators can make space for student voices to impact decisions.

8. **Which adults should have agency in school decisions?** Too often, parents and teachers find themselves at the mercy of their school systems. Should they have more power and influence in school decisions that impact them and their families? In this chapter, leaders explore how schools could and should vest power outside of traditional administrative structures.

9. **Will school ever be enough to change someone's trajectory?** From housing, to the world of work, and to parent and family needs, what role should schools play to effectively support young people for long-term success? In this chapter, leaders explore multi-sector responses to students' needs.

The goal of *One Good Question* is to help us think about how to transform public education in our communities so that all kids get the education they deserve. Regardless of your professional role, your parental status, or whether you had a positive experience in school, we all have a vested interest in education outcomes. One of the things that I learned working in schools across the United States is that many of our problems are painfully similar. In each new city where I worked, people would tell me how dire the education was, and how local systemic barriers were contributing to this. Over time, I was able to identify which concerns were common (racial and economic disparities, generational trauma, redlining and housing segregation, school selection as social status, teacher quality, teacher diversity, funding disparities) and which were more regional (racial and ethnic composition, industry-related access to jobs, local legislation, local leadership vision). Each of these themes, if explored in your local context, could lead you to completely different examples and conclusions. That is the power of the questioning methodology.

How to interact with the book

I didn't set out to write this as a book. I was learning so much from the interviews and blog series that I was content to think of each section as its own distinct wondering. As I started considering *One Good Question* the book, Jarvis DeBerry had just published an anthology of his columns from the Times-Picayune. He encouraged me to think about the story that I wanted to tell with this body of work. That's what I've done — to use *One Good Question* as an invitation into how my personal and professional lives colored my own understanding of the challenges in informal and formal education. Every now and then someone would ask me how I would answer my own question. This book is my answer.

That said, I respect non-sequential learning. Maybe you start by reading the chapter with the questions that are most interesting to you, or you may start by reading individual interviews. A word to the wise — just because a chapter is labeled with "language," for example, does not mean that it is the only chapter where interviews address issues of multilingualism in education. There is an appendix at the end of the book to track themes across all of the articles, so you may want to start there. Whichever path you choose, I encourage you to think about your own answer to the original "one good question": What experiences are you bringing to this question? What is it that you want to learn?

As you read *One Good Question*, you'll notice that the voice and language used change with each interview. That's intentional. Instead of redacting other leaders' thoughts to my voice, I wrote each piece like an extended quote. I want you to imagine that you are in conversation with these leaders. Each of them speaks about the complexities of education from their perspective. While conducting these interviews, I learned a lot about how people discuss education in other countries — different vocabulary, different assumptions, and different acronyms. I've included definitions and footnotes to make some of the jargon clearer, but I also encourage you to try to make meaning as you're reading along. What might it mean when someone refers to English-medium education? What is the equivalent of pre-primary in your community? What are examples of tertiary education institutions?

At the end of each chapter, I invite you to reflect on what questions these interviews raised for you. The one good question that each person asks at the end of their interview isn't always directly related to the rest of their conversation. Having the space to question and consider things from different perspectives often leads us to unanticipated wonder. What is your one good question?

EDUCATION 2030: WHERE ARE WE HEADED?

CHAPTER 1

S USTAINABLE DEVELOPMENT GOALS. SDGS. What does that phrase mean to you? Unbeknownst to me, at the time that I was designing this blog series in 2015, the United Nations was hosting a historic convening on the future of the world. At their 2015 Summit, they released "Transforming Our World: The 2030 Agenda for Sustainable Development," a set of collective goals for their 193 Member States to address over the next fifteen years:

> It is a roadmap to ending global poverty, building a life of dignity for all and leaving no one behind. It is also a clarion call to work in partnership and intensify efforts to share prosperity, empower people's livelihoods, ensure peace and heal our planet for the benefit of this and future generations.
>
> - United Nations Secretary-General Ban Ki-moon

Essentially, the SDGs continued a practice of mutual accountability and public accountability for how member countries in the United Nations would approach key global issues. I consider myself a worldly person, an armchair anthropologist, and a traveler. I started the blog after I had founded and led a network of language immersion and International Baccalaureate schools and had done an international fellowship. I thought I had some perspective on international education needs but I had no idea what the SDGs were. As I started the interviews, it became very clear that international educators and leaders not only knew what the SDGs were, but thought about how their work aligned to these global commitments for a sustainable future.

Here are the seventeen Sustainable Development Goals for 2030:

Reprinted with permission[2]. UN General Assembly, *Transforming our world: the 2030 Agenda for Sustainable Development*, 21 October 2015, A/RES/70/1, available at: https://www.un.org/sustainabledevelopment/

The pithy categories for the Sustainable Development Goals are accompanied by longer, carefully worded definitions and 169 targets that correlate to one of the goals. These goals are a set of global indicators, and individual governments have also established specific in-country indicators.

Global education leaders specifically referenced SDG 4: Quality Education, commonly called Education 2030. The first time someone referenced Education

---

[2] The content of this publication has not been approved by the United Nations and does not reflect the views of the United Nations or its officials or Member States.

2030, I had lots of follow-up questions for them. By contrast, only one US-based interviewee spoke about Education 2030 and that really stood out to me. If education leaders are having a conversation about education globally, are we even all talking about the same thing? Let's take a closer look at Sustainable Development Goal 4: Quality Education.

Reprinted with permission[3]. UN General Assembly, *Transforming our world: the 2030 Agenda for Sustainable Development*, 21 October 2015, A/RES/70/1, available at: https://www.un.org/sustainabledevelopment/

The ten targets for Education 2030 are clearly based on intersectional perspectives and data analysis for our most vulnerable populations worldwide. Each of the targets specifically names gender parity as a reminder that in so many countries across the globe, girls and women don't have equal access to formal education. With these targets, the committee asserts that we can't achieve the Education 2030 goal if girls and women are left out of the equation. As I read through the ten targets, I saw how easily we could apply these same targets to our urban core and impoverished rural communities in the United States. Don't take my word for it. As you read through these targets, which ones do you think apply to your local context?

---

[3] The content of this publication has not been approved by the United Nations and does not reflect the views of the United Nations or its officials or Member States.

Table A: Leading Sustainable Development Goal (SDG) 4: Education 2030 Targets.

4.1 By 2030, ensure that all girls and boys complete free, equitable and quality primary and secondary education leading to relevant and Goal-4 effective learning outcomes.

4.2 By 2030, ensure that all girls and boys have access to quality early childhood development, care and pre-primary education so that they are ready for primary education.

4.3 By 2030, ensure equal access for all women and men to affordable and quality technical, vocational and tertiary education, including university.

4.4 By 2030, substantially increase the number of youth and adults who have relevant skills, including technical and vocational skills, for employment, decent jobs and entrepreneurship.

4.5 By 2030, eliminate gender disparities in education and ensure equal access to all levels of education and vocational training for the vulnerable, including persons with disabilities, indigenous peoples and children in vulnerable situations.

4.6 By 2030, ensure that all youth and a substantial proportion of adults, both men and women, achieve literacy and numeracy.

4.7 By 2030, ensure that all learners acquire the knowledge and skills needed to promote sustainable development, including, among others, through education for sustainable development and sustainable lifestyles, human rights, gender equality, promotion of a culture of peace and non-violence, global citizenship and appreciation of cultural diversity and of culture's contribution to sustainable development.

4.A Build and upgrade education facilities that are child, disability and gender sensitive and provide safe, nonviolent, inclusive and effective learning environments for all.

4.B By 2030, substantially expand globally the number of scholarships available to developing countries[4], in particular least developed countries, small island developing States and African countries, for enrolment in higher education, including vocational training and information and communications technology, technical, engineering and scientific programmes, in developed countries and other developing countries.

4.C By 2030, substantially increase the supply of qualified teachers, including through international cooperation for teacher training in developing countries, especially least developed countries and small island developing states.

UN General Assembly, *Transforming our world: the 2030 Agenda for Sustainable Development*, 21 October 2015, A/RES/70/1, available at: https://www.un.org/sustainabledevelopment/

Leaders reference Education 2030 throughout the book, but in this chapter, we hear from four voices rooted in the intersectional spirit of the goals. Dr. Phumzile Mlambo-Ngcuka (South Africa), UN Under-Secretary-General and Executive Director of United Nations Women, gives some context on women's equality worldwide; Zaki Hasan (Bangladesh) explores the relationship between education access and the local economy in Bangladesh; Susan Patrick (USA) raises questions about trust in US education agencies; and John Wood (USA) challenges the role of international leaders when supporting education initiatives in the global south.

---

[4] There is no one agreed upon definition of a developing country. The United Nations typically refers to developed economies, economies in transition and developing economies as defined by World Economic Situation and Prospects (WESP).

WHEN WOMEN SUCCEED, THE WORLD SUCCEEDS: DR. PHUMZILE MLAMBO-NGCUKA (SOUTH AFRICA)

I was fortunate to meet Dr. Mlambo-Ngcuka a couple of times while writing the original blog, once at the Global Network Forum for Women and again at the book launch for *This I Believe: Essays from the Men and Women of Eisenhower Fellowships*. Dr. Mlambo-Ngcuka played a different role at each event. At the Global Network Forum for Women, the setting of this first story, I was in complete awe at her brilliance, eloquence, and conviction about the world's obligation to girls and women. A little over a year later when I saw her at the book launch, the tables were turned. I was the one speaking on a panel and she was milling about the cocktail hour like regular people. I still remember my nervous fangirl moment when I asked if we could take a picture together (she said yes!). Throughout the event, she checked in with fellows from the Eisenhower Fellowship's inaugural class of leaders from sub-Saharan Africa. Seeing her greet, hug, and laugh with these leaders reminded me that her presence was not just work but another way to build community across countries and continents.

In the fall of 2015, at the opening of the Global Network Forum for Women, Dr. Phumzile Mlambo-Ngcuka, UN Under-Secretary-General and Executive Director of UN Women, presented an update on the world's priorities for women's equality worldwide. Dr. Mlambo-Ngcuka has paved the way on intersectional vision-setting that centers the needs of women and girls for decades. Before naming the new targets in the Sustainable Development Goals (SDGs), she reminded us of what has improved in women's status worldwide in the last twenty years:

- Girls' education has improved, especially in countries with the lowest levels.

- Countries have created gender machineries[5]— offices to promote gender equality.
- Lots of laws have been passed to recognize domestic violence as a crime, marital rape as a crime, to enable women to have property rights, and to amend constitutions to reflect gender equality.
- There has been some progress in maternal death and infant mortality; not where we should be, but progress still.
- More countries offer targeted health services to women.
- Countries have invested time, energy, research, and hard work in the fight against HIV and AIDS. More people living with HIV are living a full life.
- Poverty has been reduced.

If you live in a country like the US, you may wonder why these gains matter. To which Dr. Mlambo-Ngcuka offers an answer, "These efforts need to be celebrated. We have more women in visible positions of power and at the center of the UN's SDG agenda. We cannot expect the world to succeed if women are not succeeding."

While Dr. Mlambo-Ngcuka prefers the glass-half-full perspective, she was very clear that our governments are still marginalizing women's development. Governments only invest 10% of their funding towards gender equality in efforts that contribute to the sewing machine syndrome[6] in developing countries. They continue to treat women's issues like micro-enterprises instead of recognizing the major economic power and potential of more than 50% of the population. Violence against women has remained flat in the past twenty years and we've been in a complex transition from domestic violence to cyber-crimes.

What will help countries invest in girls and women?

We need to get decision makers to stop seeing women as the problem or charity case. We will not overcome inequality or poverty or achieve sustainable peace

---

[5] Usually refers to formal government structures assigned to promote gender equality and/or improve the status and rights of women.

[6] Sewing machine syndrome refers to gender equality efforts in which governments provide supplies like a sewing machine to help bring in revenue for an impoverished family, by which girls and women can "lift themselves out of poverty."

if we do not improve the lives of women. There are only twenty women heads of state in the world. If we had more female leaders we would not be in this state. Women are part of creating the world we all want. We have to invest in women. When you leave women out, you compromise the rest of the nation.

"In every generation, there is a mission that we have to fulfill. We can either betray it or fulfill it. It is in our hands by 2030 to change the world significantly. I look forward to sprinting with you in this marathon for the next 15 years."

– Dr. Phumzile Mlambo-Ngcuka

ONE GOOD QUESTION WITH ZAKI HASAN: MOVE BANGLADESH FROM FASHION ECONOMY TO THOUGHT ECONOMY (BANGLADESH)

Zaki Hasan and I first met when he was in the United States visiting schools and youth development nonprofits to inform his own nonprofit leadership. At the time, Zaki was Executive Director (ED) of Underprivileged Children's Educational Programs Bangladesh (UCEP), which provides education and technical training to young people who never enrolled in school or dropped out of primary school. Admittedly, I didn't know much about Bangladesh, so in our first conversation, we talked more about his observations and my experience in school leadership.

When he agreed to do this interview, I was excited to learn more about my one good question from his perspective. When we talk about similar youth development and technical skills programs in the United States, we are usually focused on young people who have dropped out of high school, not primary school. The entire context of UCEP's work helped me situate American education pain points in a clearer global context. Later in the book, we will hear from American educators who are trying to change school systems because we no longer serve an industrial economy. From Zaki's lens, Bangladesh currently has an industrial economy yet he still sees the traditional models as inadequate for their future.

In what ways do our investments in education reveal our beliefs about the next generation's role in the world?

If you talk about the philosophy of education, in Bangladesh, we're still like 17th century Europe — an industrial country focused on economic equities: jobs, food, survival. We're not talking about which common social values the world should have. After I earn the money in my skilled job, do I understand the value of human life in this world? Unfortunately, what happens when there is not enough employment or job security is that people turn to unethical means to survive. There must be some global values system that we should start talking about in education. Will that not be the number-one problem when we're trying to kill each other? Not from the lack of money but due to lack of accepting diversity? Who will solve this? The medical system will not. The political system will not. Only education can do this.

Bangladesh is a young country. Since the independence, I broadly categorize the generations into three: the first generation questioned the injustice and owned the country's independence, the second generation questioned autocracy and has started the journey of democracy twenty-four years back, and now the third generation is questioning our journey without a vision, and we are heading to a bright and shiny future. This journey will only be successful when our children are equally ready through education to make the journey. This generation and future generations need to understand the values that the previous generations built this country on, i.e., justice and democracy. Other values may change with time, but justice and democracy must continue to improve in order to create a society based on equity.

We need a different education investment framework and the UN's Sustainable Development Goals give us a reasonable starting point. There are some missing focuses though. For example, in the next fifteen years, when we talk about basic literacy, it has to take into account how differently we have started communicating by using technology than what it had been so far in the form of in-person communication and written scripts. The long-discussed issue of digital divide is becoming a much more complex issue in the coming days. For example, a person with postgraduate education from Bangladesh today might have less exposure to new technologies than a typical elementary school child in the US. There has to be more investment in education, especially in the methods of communication, to decrease the global achievement gap. The developed countries still have a lot to improve, but they are still focused on their immediate crisis of economic survival rather than equally having social value creation and even equally important aspects of transforming our children into thought leaders. Less developed countries need a radical restructuring of education. Bangladesh will stay stuck in factories and provide good clothes to wear, but other developing countries may continue to rise in the thought economy. We have to change the education system to allow people to think freely and creatively.

In Bangladesh, you've been instrumental in growing global education programming. How effective are western innovations/models in improving education gains in Bangladesh? Are there other US education initiatives that would advance education access?

My visits to public community schools in the US were bittersweet. Children there have an assurance that they can go to school in their area. Common Core State Standards had just been rolled out and it was wonderful to see that the federal and state systems had agreed to core common standards and still had the freedom to apply them in their own way. The most beautiful moments I had were when I observed student-teacher interactions. I visited Barack Obama Male Leadership Academy and, at first, I couldn't understand the role of the teacher and the student. Sometimes the student was leading the class and the teacher was in the back of the room. The roles seemed interchangeable and that made me happy.

Here, going to school is like winning a lottery ticket. Even if you get access to a school, you cannot assure that the quality will be maintained. In the classroom, many teachers are not trying to make learning interesting; they are trying to 'teach' children instead of making the children interested to 'learn.' Education can be important to empower students to take control of the class. The classroom environment that I saw in the US is something that was beautiful. No one wants to feel inferior, not even your three-year-old child. I don't know how it happened in the US and how it could happen in Bangladesh. If the US reached consensus on Common Core State Standards (CCSS) in 2012, maybe we can do it here by 2022. If we can shift to more inclusive pedagogy, especially children-focused learning, the next generation will believe that more is possible in all schools.

ZAKI'S ONE GOOD QUESTION: Education is about creating global peace. Are we matching what we really want to accomplish through education? Are we missing the way that education should be defined?

ONE GOOD QUESTION WITH SUSAN PATRICK: HOW CAN WE BUILD TRUST IN OUR EDUCATION SYSTEM? (USA)

All of the *One Good Question* interviews were about an hour long, but this conversation with Susan Patrick was unique because it yielded two completely different pieces. I don't think that Susan and I had met in person before the interview but I learned more about her and her work in the years that followed. In 2020, because of the COVID-19 pandemic, every educator gained experience with distance learning, telelearning, online learning platforms, and hybrid instruction delivery. Traditional educators with strong beliefs about seat time[7] found themselves questioning that assumption. Questioning traditional in-person instructional delivery, particularly with a lens towards technology integration, has been Susan's life work. As the CEO and President of the Aurora Institute, she advocates for personalized, competency-based, and blended online learning. Rereading this interview in 2021, after experiencing online learning with my own children, has given me a different appreciation for how Susan weaves together equity and inclusion as essential components for innovative instructional models.

In what ways do our investments in education reveal our beliefs about the next generation's role in the world?

There's a big difference in how you would fund the education system if you were building for the longer term — you would invest in building capacity and trust. We need to take a very honest look at our investments. If people and relationships matter, we need to be building our own sense of inquiry. That's not at odds with

---

[7] Seat time refers to how much time students spend in the classroom. Most state education funding in the US is based on seat time.

42

innovation investments. We should be about innovation with equity. That way, we can change our own perspectives while we build new solutions.

The debate about top-down education reform versus bottom-up education innovation is tied to the same trust issues. In Finland, they made an effort to go towards a trust-based model and it meant investing in educator capacity so that the systems trust educators to make the best decisions in real time. If we don't start investing in trust, we can't get anywhere.

When US educators visit other countries, we tend to look for silver bullet programs from the highest-performing countries. What are we missing in that search? During my Eisenhower Fellowship, I was able to meet with teams from Organisation for Economic Co-operation and Development (OECD) and United Nations Educational, Scientific and Cultural Organization (UNESCO) and that gave me great perspective. UNESCO publishes annual Education 2030 outlook briefs to present their global education development agenda that looks at the whole child. Their goals are broad enough to include developing nations who aren't yet educating 100% of their population. When we read through the goals and indicators, the US could learn a lot from having our current narrow focus on academics. Our current education structure is not going to lead us to provide a better society. Are we even intending to build a better society for the future? We're not asking the big questions. We're asking if students can read and do math on grade level in grades three through eight. By contrast, in Canada, they ask if a student has yet met or exceeded expectations. If students haven't yet met or exceeded expectations, then what are we doing to get them there? You don't just keep moving and allowing our kids to have gaps in knowledge.

Across the global landscape of education systems, there is a diversity of governance from top-down to bottom-up regarding system control, school autonomy and self-regulation and how this impacts processes and policies for quality assurance, evaluation, and assessments. It is important to realize the top-down and bottom-up dynamics are often a function of levels of public trust combined with transparency for data and doing what is best for all kids. In the US, let's face it, our policy conversations around equity are driven by a historical trend of a massive achievement gap. Said another way, there is a huge lack of trust from the federal government toward states, from states to districts and even down to schools and classrooms. We ask, "How do we trust that we're advancing equity in our schools?"

However, when you start to think about what we need to do to advance a world-class education for all students and broaden the definition of student success, you hit a wall in coherent policy that would align to better practices. There's so much mistrust in the system given our history of providing inequalities across the education system; it is inequitable. In recognizing that our education system isn't based on trust, therefore, perhaps we need to focus on what our ultimate goals and values for our education systems should be and then backward engineer how we get there, how we hold all parties accountable, and how we could actually build trust in a future state. We need to consider future-focused approaches that work to build trust, transparency and greater accountability, and build capacity for continuous improvement. We do need to assure comparability in testing to tell us whether we have been providing an equitable education. It's just right now, this lack of trust is creating a false dichotomy of limited approaches to a future-focused education system. We're defaulting that the only test that we trust is criterion-referenced standardized tests.

We need to take a deep look at the implications of what systems of assessments mean for the rest of the system. It seems that we're only willing to trust education outcomes based on a standardized test with which we commit to locking students into age-based cohorts, and we focus primarily on the delivery of content. What would be the long-term implications for creating better transparency, more frequent inquiry approaches on what is working best for both adults and children? Are there different ways to evaluate student work and determine whether students are building knowledge, broader skills, and competencies they need for future success? Can we consider a range of future goals and backward map alternative approaches? All assessments don't have to be norm-referenced. This is a familiar conversation with education experts globally. I'm afraid we're not having that conversation in the US.

That's what's so interesting to me about iNACOL[8] work. It's global and focuses on future states for educators and practitioners designing new models using the research on how students learn best. We listen to practitioners working on next-generation designs and then ask, "Is our policy aligned with actually doing what's best for kids?" What if you could set a vision for a profile of high school graduates that would ensure success? What goals would you want for redefining what students need to know and be able to do? And how would you then approach aligning the systems of policy and practice with

---

[8] iNACOL was renamed Aurora Institute in 2019.

what's right for kids? The new federal Every Student Succeeds Act (ESSA)[9] law gives states the flexibility to come up with new definitions of students' success. States can now use multiple measures — and still report data transparently. This is a really important time to engage in deep conversations between states and communities, families, local leaders and educators around what we would do for redefining success — but I'm not seeing yet any states that are having enough foundational conversations on the ultimate goals and vision of education WITH COMMUNITIES. I'm hearing educational leaders say, "All we know how to do is NCLB" . . . and wonder which other indicators a future accountability system might require. They're uncomfortable thinking about alternatives. It's a sort of "Stockholm Syndrome" of educational policy limited by the past. ESSA is an opportunity to engage in real dialogue with the communities we serve. Communities have been locked out of the process for years now. Community outreach has become a box that people check, but it's an ongoing dialogue and should be about building understanding and trust. This is a really rare opportunity in the United States to engage in a broader conversation around student success with local school boards and communities. This would encourage innovation and provide a clear platform driven by communities on the clear goals and outcomes we hope to achieve in our education system for equity and excellence.

When I think about one good question, I'm clear that who asks the question is as pertinent as which questions they ask. Earlier, I mentioned that investment in the long-term capacity building of our education system would require building our own sense of inquiry. In other more top-down nationalistic approaches to education in countries outside the US, leaders do control the system, so they are having strong "values-based" conversations about education in the context of societal goals, too. Because we have a strong federalist approach to education, the US Department of Education doesn't have a federal role in that way, and quite frankly, we can't have a national or even state-level values-based conversation in the same way. In a federalist approach, we have 13,600 school boards with local control. The unit of change in this country is the local school district. School leaders, superintendents, charter management organization (CMO) leaders — they actually can drive the values

---

[9] The Every Student Succeeds Act was signed into law in December 2015 and replaced the previous US education law No Child Left Behind.

conversation about what our educational goals, vision, and values are and how we measure success transparently. We've stopped talking about values in the name of objectives related to literacy and numeracy. I believe literacy and numeracy are extremely important, but let's not forget that the foundation for reading and arithmetic (with all students having proficiency) is not enough in the modern world. For students to be successful it is a "yes, and . . ." with literacy and numeracy being important content but not enough for a full education. I don't know how schools can address the extreme inequities in our education without having a values conversation and a reframing of conversations around redefining student success with broader definitions of student success.

SUSAN'S ONE GOOD QUESTION: I think that our local communities should start asking themselves these two questions:

- When a student graduates what should they know and be able to do?

- What is our definition of student success?

ONE GOOD QUESTION WITH JOHN WOOD: TEACHING THE WORLD TO READ (USA)

In the introduction, I mention that some of these interviews resulted from a cold call or random email request. John Wood was one of those! The only time that we have crossed paths in real life was across a crowded tent one year at the Aspen Action Forum. I had learned about Room to Read and their work on global literacy with deep local leadership and wanted to know more. John founded Room to Read after an early career at Microsoft and when I interviewed him, he was still the CEO — working on strategy, fund development, and public brand. I'm pretty sure John was in a taxi somewhere in Shanghai during our call and I appreciate that he made time to wonder with me. Sidenote: if you're waiting for permission to reach out to a stranger to advance your next project, your one good question, your great idea, here it is.

In what ways do our investments in education reveal our beliefs about the next generation's role in the world?

Room to Read was founded in 2000 as a little unknown startup. We boil our belief down to six simple words: World change starts with educated children. We truly believe that if you want to change the future, the biggest no brainer in the world, you start with educating your children. Traditionally, for parents, that means your own children. Those who have been given the gift of education then have an obligation to give back to kids in low-income countries. We have a duty to give back and an opportunity to change things forever. We all have an ancestor who was the one to break the cycle of poverty for our family. Once that cycle is broken, the benefit pays forward for generations. To me, you look at the world today with over 100,000,000 children not in schools and two-thirds are girls and women. If you want to change the world, then education is the smartest place to start.

Literacy and primary education have a dramatic positive impact on life expectancy, overall health, and ending the cycle of extreme poverty in

developing nations. **Beyond making books and reading accessible, the Room to Read model has created complex local education ecosystems that are highly responsive to local needs. What else does the ecosystem need to be sustainable for all children?**

One of the most important things is that the communities we work with are fully invested in each and every project that we do. It's not plunking something down for them to use, but co-building something the community is co-invested in. We also need the government to be co-invested in the projects and have some skin in the game as well. Our model is one of local employees, it's not Americans flying over to do durable projects and telling local people what to do. It's a local community buy-in as employees, volunteers, parents in the planning committee, and then the government providing the teachers and the librarians and paying their salaries. As a result of that ecosystem, and we have the data to prove it, the model is more sustainable over time.

How are you getting government engagement? What strategies could other international education NGOs adopt?

For us, we had to prove that we had a scalable model. Government doesn't want to work with an NGO unless they have a big vision, a scalable model, resources, and can impact the target population on a serious scale. That's what we've been able to deliver with the governments. Too many folks want to do one-off projects. What we're saying is that we can impact change at the town, region, and even national level.

> **JOHN'S ONE GOOD QUESTION:** If we know that education is the best way to change the future, and to impact subsequent generations, then why is the world not doing more about the fact that more than 750 million people lack basic literacy?

How will you know when you have *your* one good question?

At the end of each chapter, I offer some guidance to help you develop your one good question. The ultimate test is, can you take this question to a different person, different community, different sector and learn about the most pressing needs from their perspective? Let's reconsider the Education 2030 targets in the Sustainable Development Goals. For the Education 2030 targets to be effective, they need to create enough space for each country to respond with locally relevant data and strategies. It's important to identify a couple of known variables in the question that you're asking. In this example, the first known variable could be: Who would be the beneficiary of the Education 2030 question? Answer: Member countries and nations. All solutions must lead to strengthened outcomes for the entire country, not just a region or specific population. Each Education 2030 target makes very explicit connections between education access and gender parity. So the second known variable could be the hypothesis that, when girls and women have more access to education and employment, they improve local economies. One good question might ask: What conditions need to be true for girls and women to have an outsized impact on their local economy?

In the United States, access to formal education for girls and boys is fairly equitable, but what the Education 2030 targets require is that we track access and outcomes through career. In 2020, as a result of the global COVID-19 pandemic, it was estimated that nearly three million women in the United States left the workforce.[10] Both the International Monetary Fund (IMF) and The World Bank advise that investing in women in the workforce is a key component to grow the economy, yet the United States is facing the lowest levels of women in the workplace since the 1980s. What contributed to this exodus? Women left the workplace at a higher rate than men because women still consistently shoulder a larger burden of family care responsibilities. This exodus disproportionately impacted Black and Latina women. Community leaders across the US have had

---

[10] US Bureau of Labor Statistics. 2020 Women in the Workplace Study - McKinsey & LeanIn. org. https://www.cbsnews.com/news/covid-crisis-3-million-women-labor-force/

to redesign public life because of the global pandemic. In those redesign efforts, have any of those leaders asked questions about the particular experiences of Black and Latina women in the workplace? What might be different about your community solutions if these types of questions were pervasive in every planning conversation?

WHAT ARE YOU WONDERING?

ZAKI WONDERS: Education is about creating global peace. Are we matching what we really want to accomplish through education? Are we missing the way that education should be defined?

SUSAN WONDERS: I think that our local communities should start asking themselves these two questions:

- When a student graduates, what should they know and be able to do?
- What is our definition of student success?

JOHN WONDERS: If we know that education is the best way to change the future, and to impact subsequent generations, then why is the world not doing more about the fact that more than 750 million people lack basic literacy?

When you think about long-term community education goals, like the targets in Education 2030, what comes to mind? What did you already know about education outcomes that was challenged by this chapter?

As you reflect on your one good question —

- Think about your audience: Which voices were missing from this chapter? Who are the experts for your wondering?
- Think about your context: What about the Education 2030 targets would matter most for your local needs?
- Think about your timing: Are you trying to get clarity on what has occurred or on what could be?

ARE YOU PREPARING YOUR STUDENTS TO BECOME YOUR PEERS?

CHAPTER 2

N THE SUMMER OF 2006, I moved my family from Brooklyn, New York, to St. Louis, Missouri, and began searching for the right learning community for my children and myself. On the heels of teaching in the Middle Years Programme (MYP) and Diploma Programme (DP) of the International Baccalaureate, I was frustrated with most traditional school models. I found that most urban schools were expecting Black and Brown students, especially those from low socioeconomic communities, to consume knowledge and not inform it. I started my own inquiry into school design. What if we offered the most engaging, academically rigorous education to an intentionally diverse community and made it free for all students? What if all children had access to the same education as the children of world leaders? What if they all learned to be proud of their bilingualism and saw the world through multiple perspectives? What if they saw themselves as change agents in their communities now instead of waiting for others or older versions of themselves to take action? This is what I wanted to create — an environment where young people were supported to make changes that mattered to them, and where adults supported students and respected their ideas. I was able to bring my vision to life when I founded the St. Louis Language Immersion Schools (SLLIS) in 2007.

At age seventeen, I had my first taste of that kind of trust and respect for youth voice. In the summer between junior year and senior year of high school, I taught summer school courses to middle schoolers. My mentors were nineteen-year-old college undergrads and they taught me what it meant for my voice to matter. At seventeen, I was reserved and observant, yet these adults trusted me and trusted my perspective. That experience cemented the idea of youth voice for me. As I continued my teaching career, I was focused on how we can release ourselves from the teacher-student hierarchy and make space for students to inform their own learning. How could I release my own fears or worries about how students would lead? How could I cultivate a co-learning environment, where students saw themselves and their peers as educators? As a teacher in my twenties, I worked with middle and high school students, so there were times when our age difference felt more like a peer relationship. When I started the school network in St. Louis, though, I was in my thirties and our students were all elementary aged. My vision for student agency challenged a lot of adults who thought our students were too young to be trusted or that they lacked sophisticated analysis in their work. A few years ago, I shared this example of SLLIS' student work with the International Baccalaureate Organization[11].

"One of our first fifth grade exhibitions opened with a student from The Spanish School asking about fear. She began with a pie chart that revealed the most common fears: clowns, barking dogs, abandoned houses, and scary movies. Number one fear? Abandoned houses. Then she adeptly shifted to a map of GIS data depicting the number of abandoned houses in our city and shared her first conclusion: this means that people are afraid to visit my neighborhood, and residents may be afraid to come home. She then linked the census tract with the highest concentration of blighted property and correlated it to personal crime that revealed higher rates of crime in these neighborhoods as well. She continued with examples of the same phenomenon in other urban areas across the country. What can we do about it? Invest in neighborhoods with services — fill the vacant properties with schools, community centers, art projects, and give people something to come home to, all in the name of reducing their fears about urban communities."

[11] Broussard, Rhonda "Developing Student Agency Improves Equity and Access" The IB Community Blog. November 14, 2015. https://blogs.ibo.org/blog/2015/11/14/developing-student-agency-improves-equity-and-access/

Literally, *Are You Smarter Than a 5th Grader?* was playing out in our school's multipurpose room. These young people were asking questions and providing an analysis that rivaled adult work.

That's what this chapter is about — what are the ways in which we're creating space and expectations for youth to be our learning peers? Darren Isom (USA) explores the tension between letting kids be kids and youth development. Chris Plutte (USA) addresses peacebuilding and the roles that youth have, can have, and should have in peace movements worldwide. Ejaj Ahmad (Bangladesh) asks what happens if we redefine leadership as an activity and not as a title, would more youth take up the mantle? Vania Masias (Peru) shares what happens when adults, even young, cool, connected adults, step aside and let youth lead.

ONE GOOD QUESTION WITH DARREN ISOM: ARE YOU PREPARING YOUR STUDENTS TO BECOME YOUR PEERS? (USA)

Darren Isom and I sat on the front porch of a Memphis home overlooking Overton Park, and before we could even begin this interview, we made space to honor how our friendship and professional respect have deepened over the course of our thirty-year relationship. We met as teenage staffers at Summerbridge in New Orleans. Darren went on to build his career in youth development and consulting, and I went on to the more traditional educator route. We zigzagged across the country and a couple of continents for work, studies, sometimes love, and vowed to stay in each other's lives. In 2016, Darren had just hired his founding team at Memphis Music Initiative, and I was helping his team identify how to operationalize their values. We took a break from their team retreat to let our minds wander together for this interview.

If you've ever met Darren, you know that he is a *raconteur*. And at multiple times during our interview, we both said, "We should be recording this." I took a couple of portraits of him on the porch instead. What amazed me about our conversation was how I learned new things about Darren's work and perspective because of *my* one good question. As you're developing your question, don't assume that you know how anyone will answer. It was really a gift to see youth development through Darren's eyes.

In what ways do our investments in education reveal our beliefs about the next generation's role in the world?

I back away from the "education" conversation because I think of my work as more about youth development than formal schooling. The pivotal and catalytic moments in my own learning and development happened outside of the regular school day. Even though I attended rigorous academic institutions throughout my life, it was my out-of-school experiences, often afterschool and summer activities and programs, that offered me the opportunities to suture my academic experiences and make them real and relevant. I recognized my talent for writing outside of school and recognized my ability to lead and manage via summers working at Summerbridge/Breakthrough Collaborative. We spend so much time thinking about academic performance and that comes from a place of privilege. When you're white and privileged, all you must do is to be smart to succeed. When you're Black, privileged or otherwise, you recognize that being smart is necessary but not sufficient. Being able to navigate the world successfully and achieve both professionally and personally requires more than academic preparation. I'm not saying we should downplay the role of academics, clearly they are critical, but we can't sell kids this false promise that being smart is all that you need. Youth development makes kids fuller — it gives them the tools they need to navigate the world with those smarts.

Our education perspectives are really based on the education that we received, which then informs what we see as the drivers of success. What we need to be asking ourselves is "What actual role do we want our youth to play in the world?" I educate the kids in our program expecting them to become my personal and professional peers. I remember when my first student from Summerbridge went to Howard, my alma mater, a fellow white teacher said "Isn't that impressive! Did you ever think that she could go to Howard?" And I replied, "That was the whole point of our working with her, no?" We have in many ways these unarticulated hierarchies that manifest themselves in our expectations of our students. Even when we're serving kids to help them academically, we don't do so with the belief that they'll become our peers. We do so with the expectation that they'll "do well for their setting." I feel very strongly about upward mobility. That's what America has meant for me and my family. I don't just believe in it, but I think that certain kids have obligations to it — folks are counting on them. We're raising these kids with the expectation that they're going to do magic — jumping numerous social tiers and integrating and succeeding in worlds their parents didn't even know existed. If we expect them to do magic, we have to be prepared to give them the tools, tricks, and confidence they need to do so successfully. I worry that we are encouraging our Black kids, our gay kids, our poor kids to literally cover elements of their beauty for the sake of integrating. We are giving them one path to success and forcing them to abandon their uniqueness, their greatest asset, to get there.

It's become common for schools to position arts programs as support for academic gains (i.e., music improves math), but is that the most important function of arts education?

Kids should be allowed to be kids. You have your whole life to be an adult and adulting ain't fun or easy. I'm a cinephile and the theme that always gets me crying is when kids are forced into adult situations at a young age, like in the Italian film *La vita è bella (Life is Beautiful).* Those situations are just so unfair. Life is tough and you should have a good fifteen years where you can be a child. There's something to be said about giving kids space to be playful and young and youthful. We must give children a space to dream before we start telling them what they can't do. You'll spend your whole life with people telling you what you need to be, what you can't do, where you can sit, where you can live. Can you have some years to push the boundaries? Children excel at having fun. It's an asset. We should leverage it.

At Memphis Music Initiative, we give kids fun, meaningful, high-quality music opportunities. Very often we go into Black and Brown schools with well-meaning white boards and leadership and when we talk about what we're trying to achieve, they'll say "That sounds great, but we don't want to distract the kids from academic learning with music and arts." It's problematic because these same rich, white folks would never be on the board of [insert fancy private school here] and characterize arts and music education as a distraction.

In youth development, we should be working to create the world that we want our own children to be in, not a world for somebody else's poor children. You have to think about it selfishly. Seeing music and arts engagement as a "distraction" speaks to a disconnect in how communities experience art. Wealthy families see art as a distraction, a way to fill your free time, an activity of leisure. As Black Americans — wealthy or not — art is much more than that. It's the way we navigate life, diffuse anger, celebrate successes — it's a way of creating beauty in a world that's often everything but. A white home without music or art is simply bland or boring. A Black home without music or art is without joy. Our ability to give our kids these opportunities is necessary in their development, critical to their joy.

An organization that I admire is the Sesame Street Foundation. I've been enamored by their campaign to send puppet trucks to refugee camps as part of their belief that children have the right to be children no matter what their situation is, and that the most dire and desperate situations only mandate these youthful opportunities for youth. There's a recent article questioning when schools became such joyless places that resonated so strongly for me. As a child, I loved school, my school and teachers loved me. I was good at school and my teachers did a stellar job of creating a protective environment for me — an awkward, nerdy, gay kid. As educational elites, we're so busy experimenting with what schools for poor Black kids should look like. I just find all the experimentation really confusing. We're experimenting when we actually know what works. Why don't we recreate for them the type of education that we had growing up? The kind that worked for us? The kind that made us smart, empowered, and world ready? Are they not worthy of it? Do we think that they can't digest it? I recognize that education reformers would say that we haven't changed schools since Rip Van Winkle, and question what we should be doing differently to prepare kids for a fast-changing world and not handicap them. But what's fundamentally broken? Is it the model or the implementation that's failed?

DARREN'S ONE GOOD QUESTION: How do we support our youth to manifest their beauty? How do we enable young people to embrace and showcase that thing of beauty while readying the world to accept and embrace it?

ONE GOOD QUESTION WITH CHRIS PLUTTE: CAN GLOBAL UNDERSTANDING HELP US ADDRESS RACE ISSUES IN THE UNITED STATES? (USA)

By the time Chris Plutte and I scheduled this interview, I had a glimpse into his perspective. Chris was the Founder and Executive Director of Global Nomads Group and we met through the Pahara Institute, a fellowship of education reform leaders in the United States. We joked that the fellowship organizers intentionally sprinkled in those of us with more global perspectives to balance out a US-centric approach to education. But as I learned early on in the one good question process, American perspectives on global education are quite different from the people who were actually raised in the education system in their country. In this interview, we learn how exposure to global partnership can impact what American students learn from their international counterparts. At the end of each chapter I ask a few reflection questions about the content and your own wondering. Two reflection questions stand out to me from Chris' interview: Which voices were missing from this chapter? Who are the experts for your wondering? I find myself wondering what the lessons learned would be from the youth participants in Pakistan and Palestine.

In what ways do our investments in education reveal our beliefs about the next generation's role in the world?

There's a genuine interest in wanting to be global citizens, but folks don't know where to start. When you ask someone how they're working towards the goals of being global citizens, there are very few examples. Programs like Global Nomads Group are still a "current event" on a Friday at 1pm. That's how American schools "go global." I don't think we're preparing kids for a global society at all. We're failing at that. We are thinking about right now, but not 2030 or 2045 when we'll be more connected than we already are. We're not teaching the kids skills of communication and collaboration across countries. There's a shift that needs to happen from competition against Finland and Singapore to collaboration with Finland and Singapore. Then we need to work backwards with the skills that young people need to develop for that new economy.

Personally, I come to this from a peace-building lens. How do you bring people together who don't understand each other and are in perceived conflict with each other? We live in a world where people bounce up against each other and don't have the skills to navigate that. Ten to fifteen years ago, we had American diplomats sitting in foreign capitals representing American values and cultures to other communities. We're now working side-by-side and engaging, but we don't know how to do intercultural communication. We won't be able to do that until we engage whole communities, parents, and educators to become global citizens. Give them the tools, experience, and opportunities to inquire about how the world is outside of their own city. Then they can be inspired to share those with the young people that they're educating. The investment is really with the adults right now as much as with the students.

You're the first American educator in this interview series to bring up peace as a function of education. When we talk about race, there's an inherent conversation there about peace because we're looking for peace within our communities. I'm curious about how global [perspective] can help local [solutions]. I'm stuck on Einstein's idea that no problem can be solved in the conditions in which it was created — the idea that you have to leave the environment to solve the problem. I wonder if there's an opportunity to expand on that and talk about race issues and conflict issues. There's such massive Islamophobia in the US. At Global Nomads Group, we focus on linking US schools and Muslim-majority countries. Part of the model is building compassion and empathy for one another. That's a muscle that gets developed. It's perhaps easier for suburban white kids to have a conversation around Islamophobia than race issues in their own community. Can you build that muscle globally and then pivot and use it to address race issues in the US? As an organization, we're trying to explore that possibility.

When we think of global citizenship in the US, we think about preparing Americans to be global citizens. But you can't be a global citizen by yourself.

There's a perspective called *ubuntu* — I am me because you are you. You need the "other" to be a global citizen. Right now, the American perspective on global citizenship is about taking — "How can we take from other places to be global?" Global citizenship is not about taking from other people and cultures. It's about navigating within an ecosystem with others who are also global citizens and navigating yourself with different experiences. It's a long play. It has to be cultivated and integrated over years.

What are the first steps to change? I need to articulate to people what the world actually is and be a bit of a futurist. When the educator or administrator sees themselves as a global citizen, then they can champion it. Peace Corps alumni, army brats, and third culture kids[12] seek out Global Nomad Group to impact their classrooms. The big question is how do you move beyond those converted communities and get the larger community engaged in demanding it? That's what we need right now. We need larger communities demanding it for their children and their schools in an authentic way.

So many educators in urban settings regard this work as esoteric or enrichment. How do you start from that perspective? Where we are, you have to work with the willing — networks, districts, and charters who are willing to partner with you and can be an example to others. People need to be able to have some type of anchors and understand that they can do that too. I certainly felt in my Aspen Institute fellowship that I was with these rockstar educators who are trying to get kids to graduate high school. Who am I to say, "By the way, you should also go global." I struggle with this. We have a problem here in the United States, but in comparison to rural schools in developing countries that meet under trees in the blistering sun, we also live an extraordinary opportunity. We can create a community in which people are engaging globally, and that will help their local communities. That's how I approach it with those folks: Problem solving. If you weave together problem solving, peacebuilding, and race issues, that collective lens will resonate with the education reform community. This won't recruit everyone to a global citizenship perspective, but I hope it would create enough entry points to move our work away from being on the fringe in order to get a small place at the table. And we need those entry points right now.

---

[12] Children raised in a culture or country different than their parents

With the nonprofit that you founded, Global Nomads Group, you answered one of the fundamental questions about access to get youth in developing nations connected with their global peers. What student-led actions are you seeing for youth on both sides of the experience as a result of their participation?

All our programs are project-based, so when you're paired with a school, you have to identify a problem within your community that you're going to help answer based on this program. We had a group in Pakistan focus on girls' education and girls in their community not going to school. In the US, students focused on a recycling and environmental program for trash in their community. The schools work together to compare and contrast their projects and offer ideas to each other. The results for the students in Pakistan were that they actually did a community awareness campaign about girls' education, met with families of the girls, raised money, and got scholarships for local schools to get the girls enrolled in schools. Just last week, a US school that is connected in Gaza actually planned a whole week to do a program around educating their community on Islam. The action was really inspired by the young people in the US hearing from their Palestinian counterparts on how their own stereotypes and stigmas impacted their community.

> **CHRIS' ONE GOOD QUESTION:** How do I get global citizenship to be as important as trigonometry? How do I get the broader education reform community to engage and demand global citizenship for all students?

ONE GOOD QUESTION WITH EJAJ AHMAD: WHY WE SHOULD BUILD LEADERSHIP INSTEAD OF LEADERS (BANGLADESH)

I've said before that my favorite part of conducting this interview series was when the conversation took an unanticipated turn. Talking with Ejaj Ahmad, Founder and Executive Director of the Bangladesh Youth Leadership Center, was less about the unanticipated turn and more about how it shifted my perspective on postcolonial culture. When I was preparing to open The French School and The Spanish School, I knew what kind of ethnic and cultural tensions to anticipate. France and Spain were contemporary colonial powers that carved up Africa, North and South America, and extracted local resources, exterminated indigenous communities, forced hundreds of thousands of Africans into enslavement, and in the 1960s negotiated the terms of independence and neocolonial power. I was accustomed to those conversations about French, Spanish, and even Portuguese colonization, but as an American, my understanding of British colonial rule ended centuries ago. American education leaders rarely refer to postcolonialism as a factor in school design. I was floored when Ejaj Ahmad situated the need for his youth development model in Bangladesh's postcolonial context.

In what ways do our investments in education reveal our beliefs about the next generation's role in the world?

Bangladesh became independent in 1971, and while the founding leaders were visionaries, I'm not sure they thought deeply about the kind of education that the next generation would need to take the country forward. That's my gut feeling. Once you ask this one good question, you are forced to somehow link your input and process with the output that you're seeking. As a country, we have not yet really explored the educational foundation that we need to put in place to create an inclusive and just society. I say this because we see every day how the divided education system, namely English medium (British curriculum), Bangla medium (national curriculum) and Madrassa (Islamic studies curriculum), contributes to communal tension and violent politics. Young people from these divergent education streams grow up with differing values and ideologies and they rarely interact with people from other educational backgrounds. This is one of the root causes of many of the divisions we see in Bangladesh today. Moreover, the curriculum in school, college, and university relies primarily on rote learning which doesn't foster creativity and critical thinking in students. As a result, most young people enter the job market with little prior training in problem solving.

At Bangladesh Youth Leadership Center, we aspire to see the next generation exhibit values of inclusiveness, tolerance, and compassion. We also want to see them develop strong critical thinking skills so that they can question deeply held values and assumptions. Therefore, our organization runs after-school leadership programs that unite high school, college, and university students from the three different educational systems; provide them problem solving, leadership, and communication skills; and engage them in the community where they can translate their learning into action by designing and implementing service projects.

You are committed to developing youth leadership and agency. Why does it matter?

This question is powerful because more than 52% of Bangladesh's population of 160 million is below the age of twenty-five. Traditionally, we have always equated leadership with position. We use the words 'leader' and 'leadership' interchangeably although intuitively we know that they are not the same. Leader is a person or a title, whereas leadership is an activity, which can be exercised from a position of authority or without a position of authority. If every single young person perceived leadership as an activity and not as a position, imagine the impact this shift in thinking can have in society. Young people don't have titles and they don't occupy public office. However, if they believe that they don't need a title to exercise leadership and bring change, then this sense of agency can have a tremendous impact on society. We will no longer be waiting for elected officials to solve our problems; we can take ownership of our part of the problem and do our bit to make progress in our community.

Our youth leadership programs also take young people on a journey of self-exploration, which we also feel is critical for the world today. We need to help young people ask difficult questions, reconcile multiple identities and work across religious and cultural boundaries. This is especially relevant in today's world where most of our conflicts happen due to differing values and identities. Yes, you are a Bangladeshi, or an Indian, or an American. But you are also a human being. What does it mean to be a human being in the 21st century? What are some of the values that we can all share across nationalities, cultures, and religions? I believe that good leadership education can make people curious and humble. If we can all learn to reframe our truths as assumptions and not hold a monopoly on what we believe to be true, I think we can do a better job of getting along with each other despite our differences.

EJAJ'S ONE GOOD QUESTION: Which part of our cultural DNA do we need to preserve, and which part do we need to discard to create a better world, both for us and for the ones we love?

ONE GOOD QUESTION WITH VANIA MASIAS: HOW TO DISRUPT THE VICTIM MENTALITY WHEN INVESTING IN YOUTH AGENCY (PERU)

I saw Vania Masias' work before we ever spoke. I went to a performance by Angeles D1 (pronounced *de uno*) in Miami and was deeply moved by their fusion of folkloric and contemporary dance, the historic narrative that they told through movement. As a Black woman in the diaspora and a student of traditional and folkloric dance, I'm intensely curious about how we respect traditional dance forms and honor the creative energy of contemporary dancers. There's a whole other "one good question" in here — maybe that's where my next interview series will lead us.

What Vania Masias has developed in Peru — a cultural association to lead social change — started as a dance program. Vania was, after all, a classically trained dancer who wanted to share her gifts with less-fortunate youth. What D1 has become — a movement with three different leadership tracks — is a testament to the power of inquiry. Keep reading to learn what questions Vania asked of her own work to make that shift.

In what ways do our investments in education reveal our beliefs about the next generation's role in the world?

One of my dreams is that our arts methodology becomes public policy in the public schools in my country. That's my dream because every day I see the empowerment that our youth leaders have thanks to dance or arts. I think the government, and people who have never danced, have no idea how powerful this tool is. I just came back from Trujillo, another state in Peru. I went with one of the "kids" who is 21 and has been with Angeles D1 for five years. Five years ago, he was in a gang. He finished his public school, but school gave nothing to him. He was emotionally devastated. He was into drugs, gangs, and jail. Today, he just did a TEDx talk and he's a leader of more than 200 kids in one of the most difficult communities in our region. He is a teacher and one of the best dancers in our company. He learned to know himself and to start loving himself just as he is. When you dance you are just you — you are not your name, the daughter of so-and-so, the girl that went to this school. When I dance, I am not in a social level, it's just me, my soul, myself, my truth. That's really powerful.

If I were to tell people where to invest in education, I'd say: creativity, culture, arts. I believe, because I dance and I choreograph, that every human being is a jewel. We are so beautiful on the inside, and through arts, it's a beautiful thing to bring that beauty out. Our education system was focused on the British empire, and that established norms around knowledge. In that system, if you're not good with math or literature, you're kind of a pariah. At Angeles D1, our focused education gives empowerment to the kids so teachers can see their potential and bring it out. The arts allow you to bring those other gifts to the forefront.

The Angeles D1 model has been heavily informed by the youth participants, their needs and vision. Your lessons on youth agency were very organic. How would you recommend that adults planning programs for marginalized youth intentionally incorporate these lessons into their work?

The first advice I will give is to get rid of guilt. Growing up in a country where you have everything and then you see others who have nothing, that's difficult. One big mistake I made when I started the program was that I thought I had to give everything to the youth without asking anything in return. That mentality creates beggars and welfare dependency. Don't give the toys, teach them how to make the toys so that, afterwards, they can make it and sell it and it's a development. Otherwise, they will say, "Poor me, I'm a victim," and they will keep begging. You further the stigma that says you are poor, you won't make it, so I'm solving your life. I had to learn that, and it was kind of difficult. I felt guilt all the time and they knew that. It was not healthy.

I remember one day when four or five of the first-generation dancers started stealing from the company. That day, everything changed. They weren't stealing things, they stole the choreography that we made as a group, and they went somewhere else and charged for it. I kicked them out of the group because that didn't respect D1 values. Last week, on the way to Trujillo for the TEDx talk, we saw the same kids who stole from us. They were in the exact same place, dancing under the same street light that they were ten years ago. I just turned and looked at our youth leader and started crying. OMG. There we were, a few blocks from the airport and he's going to speak to a crowd of 200 professionals about his work, yet we saw his peers in the exact same place. We said nothing to each other. It was evident. They made the decision to not grow. They wanted that life. They just wanted to stay there. It's not wrong. It's not good. It's just their decision.

When we want to communicate, we only see our side of things. A question that helped me was, "How can I reach them and generate confidence?" I decided to go through urban culture to reach our youth. I put myself in their place. I tried to see what they are looking at and understand what's going on with them. I hadn't studied psychology, sociology, or anthropology to know what was going on with them. I believed in dance. When they moved, they were communicating something to me. So with that information, I could understand what they were seeing. They put their eyes always down, they would never look at me. That gave me a lot of information and then I designed everything around that. Let's do clowning and get them to feel ridiculous. We never saw the other; to see and look is different. We're in such a rush, we never see each other. When that happened, when we really saw each other, everything changed.

> **VANIA'S ONE GOOD QUESTION:** As social organizations, can we develop the leaders of tomorrow to be pure and uncorrupted?

WHAT ARE YOU WONDERING?

DARREN WONDERS: How do we support our youth to manifest their beauty? How do we enable kids to embrace and showcase that thing of beauty while readying the world to accept and embrace it?

CHRIS WONDERS: How do I get global citizenship to be as important as trigonometry? How do I get the broader education reform community to engage and demand global citizenship for all students?

EJAJ WONDERS: Which part of our cultural DNA do we need to preserve, and which part do we need to discard to create a better world, both for us and for the ones we love?

VANIA WONDERS: As social organizations, can we develop the leaders of tomorrow to be pure and uncorrupted?

When you think about youth leadership, especially as it exists outside of formal education context, what comes to mind? What did you already know about youth development that the perspectives in this chapter challenged?

As you reflect on your one good question —

- Think about your audience: Which voices were missing from this chapter? Who are the experts for your wondering?
- Think about your context: What about youth leadership development would matter most for your local needs?
- Think about your timing: Are you trying to get clarity on what has occurred or on what could be?

WHO IS FOLLOWING THE MONEY?

CHAPTER 3

Y ONE GOOD QUESTION is essentially a question about economics: In what ways do our investments in education reveal our beliefs about the next generation's role in the world? When I posed this question to educators who were closer to the programmatic side of investment — like school and system leaders, curriculum developers, nonprofit leaders who worked directly with young people — they interpreted investment more holistically. They spoke about time, resources, staffing, and policy decisions. Some of them spoke more philosophically about how we incentivize learning activities and individual learners. As a former school system leader, their interpretations resonated with me. At the start of this interview series, I thought about investment in a very similar way.

In early 2016, I had a brief conversation with an education funder that fundamentally shifted how I understood education investments. We had just attended a talk drawing parallels between the education reform movement in the US with the Civil Rights Movement, Marriage Equality Movement, and Disability Rights Movement. This funder understood the spirit of the analogies, but because education is a part of the federal budget, they disagreed about co-opting movement language. I had been working in education for more than twenty years and I couldn't have told you what the federal education budget was. I knew our school system budget and our state education budget, but rarely thought about how the federal education budget impacted our work with young people.

Table B: How much do you know about education budgets? 2019 United States Education Budgets[13]

US Department of Education - Appropriation	$81,164,807
Highest State Education Budget (New York)[14]	$24,040 per student
Lowest State Education Budget (Utah)	$7,628 per student
Average School District Budget[15,16]	$12,612 per student

U.S. and World Educational Spending[17]

In the United States, education spending falls short of benchmarks set by international organizations such as UNESCO, of which the US is a member. The nation puts 11.6% of public funding toward education, well below the international standard of 15%.

• Schools in the United States spend an average of $12,612 per pupil, which is the fifth-highest amount per pupil among the 37 other developed nations in the Organisation for Economic Co-operation and Development (OECD).

[13] US Department of Education, Budget History Tables 1980-2019, 2019 - 2021 State Budget Tables
[14] 2018 Annual Survey of School Systems Finances, US Census Bureau
[15] 2018, US Census Bureau
[16] Does not include public charter school expenditures
[17] 2018, Education Data , Author: Mel Hanson Date: 2020/10/28

• In terms of a percentage of its gross domestic product (GDP), the United States ranks twelfth among OECD members in spending on elementary education.

• The United States does not meet UNESCO's benchmark of a 15% share of total public expenditure on education.

• In terms of early childhood education, the United States is one of six countries that does not report any educational spending.

• In terms of postsecondary education, the US spends more than any other country at $33,180 per full-time student.

• Luxembourg spends US$22,700 per pupil, which is more than any of the other OECD nations spend on education.

• African nations spend the highest amount on education in terms of a percentage of GDP.

• At 4.96%, the United States spends a smaller percentage of its GDP on education than other developed nations, which average 5.59% of GDP in educational spending.

Before we can talk about how we're investing financial resources in the next generation, we have to acknowledge that our primary education investment tools in the US are inequitable. In Table B, we can see that education budgets vary greatly by state. When EdBuild analyzed education funding by school districts within the same state, they found that there was even greater variability in per-pupil funding.

"School funding systems in America are arbitrary, failing to support students in accordance with their needs. They are inequitable, often producing higher funding levels in low-need, affluent districts than in school systems serving students with greater needs. And they promote division by incentivizing and entrenching segregation along racial and economic lines. EdBuild's research has demonstrated the depth of these problems and shown the way to a better system."

- EdBuild[18]

As we see in Table B, the US is one of the countries with the highest gross domestic product (GDP), yet we still don't reach the international standard of investing 15% of our public funding into education. Problem 1: The country isn't investing enough in public education. Problem 2: The education funding is inequitably applied, exacerbating institutional racism and related economic disparities.

The leaders in this chapter spoke more about the dollars and cents of the education economy in the US. Michael DeGraff (USA) explores national incentives around STEM education. Dr. Michael Goetz (USA) questions which programmatic investments have the best outcomes for learners. Nicole de Beaufort (USA) takes on the tension between scarcity mindset and funding for early childhood education. Dan Varner (USA) pushes on our perceptions of women in the workplace and how gender bias impacts funding. Kathy Padian (USA) argues that it's not just the money, but what you do with it at the local level and who is accountable for budget management.

---

[18] edbuild.org

ONE GOOD QUESTION WITH MIKE DEGRAFF: ARE SCHOOLS DESTROYING THE MAKER MOVEMENT? (USA)

When I hopped on a call with Mike DeGraff, I had never actually seen a makerspace. I had vaguely heard about this movement and how makerspaces were the cutting edge of school design in 2015. As I understood it, the idea was to resource a room with a mix of tools — everything from traditional woodworking and shop materials to 3-D printers and laser cutters, including computer-assisted design software that allowed people to make whatever their heart desired.

A couple of years after our interview, I saw my first makerspace at my children's summer camp. Apparently, my eight-year-old son spent every free choice block at the makerspace, and on camp pick-up day, he couldn't wait to show it to me. We ambled down a lightly worn path under shade trees until we reached a little creek. I almost couldn't tell that we had reached the famed makerspace — this wooded area looked like the rest of the camp save a few freshly cut young branches on the ground. My son explained the tools they had: mostly saws, whittling knives, clamps, safety glasses. And the kinds of things they made: little bridges and walking sticks. When I asked what he enjoyed about it, he said it was the freedom to figure out what he wanted to make in real time. This freedom is the part of the maker movement that educators like Mike DeGraff wanted to protect from traditional schooling.

In what ways do our investments in education reveal our beliefs about the next generation's role in the world?

There was a call for 100,000 STEM teachers in the US, and since then there have been tons of initiatives, and related funding, to respond to the need (some say too much). UTEACH is a very constructivist-oriented teacher education program for STEM teachers that began at UT Austin and has spread across the country. Then we saw the launch of Maker Faire™ to showcase STEAM design in an informal learning space. When I went to my first Faire in 2011 or 2012, I was amazed that there wasn't tighter articulation between schools, teacher education programs, and what was going on in this sector.

In schools, "making" is mostly robotics, especially at the secondary level. School libraries may have makerspaces that are more diverse, but there's very little happening in teacher preparation for how we prepare teachers for these spaces that are proliferating. No two people have the same vision for what you mean when you say makerspace. Whenever you talk about this, it's so easy to get excited about the 3D printer, laser cutter, and other specific tools. At UTeach, we're more interested in how it transforms what kids are able to do and how teachers are empowered to teach differently. Not to dismiss the tools, but ultimately, what's so exciting about all of this stuff is how it connects to this lineage of progressive education dating back to Dewey and meaningful, authentic, relevant work. That's what's so powerful to me about this whole maker movement. It really champions student voice in a way that I don't see in any other movement/innovation/fad. How can we replicate that for every kid? One of the biggest hurdles in education and industry is to get kids curious. Makerspaces can get them to a point where they can start wondering.

The maker world and project-based formal education don't seem to respect each other enough. The maker world is super autodidactic, self-sufficient, DIY, vibrant and very curious. The maker world sentiment is that schools are going to destroy the maker movement by embracing it and standardizing it. It's not an unfounded fear. Look at the computer labs in the 1990s. Formal education succeeds in compartmentalizing learning. My biggest fear is that, if "making" becomes a part of schools, then it gets reduced to a space where you go and do "making" for an hour completely separated from (or only superficially connected to) science, math, language arts, literature, art, etc.

The formal education world is coming from a perspective that we've been doing "making" well before Maker Faire started in 2006 but have called it other things like project-based instruction. Colleges of education see the value in makerspaces, but in public education we have to focus on serving every kid. While the Maker Education Initiative motto is " every kid a maker," colleges of education and educators in general are asking what do we do with kids who aren't motivated by blinking a light or don't identify with the notion of making? How does professional development (PD) play out in these different areas and what does it look like as these spaces develop?

Do you think that schools/universities would be adopting makerspaces if it wasn't tied to funding?

These spaces have always existed in universities, but they used to be highly articulated with coursework. "Making" in a university is usually housed in the college of engineering, which makes sense for digital fabrication and electronics. You were typically a junior before you got to that level of coursework and only accessed the equipment for specific, course-related projects. If you talk to industry, a big complaint is that universities are producing engineering graduates who can calculate but can't use a screwdriver and a hammer or connect that academic experience to the real world.

A makerspace is more similar to a library type model so it's open and you can go in and make when/what you want. UT opened a Longhorn Maker Studio and when I went there in November it was full of kids making Christmas presents (like ornaments, a picture frame, and other highly personal artifacts). There's a lot of class projects, but it's more about figuring out what they can do with it. That's what's exciting.

Something that I see as very similar to the makerspace idea in the College of Natural Sciences is open inquiry, where students choose what they want to learn more about, design an experiment, and analyze results. In UTeach, one of the nine courses is totally dedicated to this process. Instructors have noticed that the hardest part of the process is to get students to become curious. Our goal is to get students to develop their own questions that can be addressed by experiments. In education, we have identified content, but the gap is how we inspire students to be curious and engaged and motivated and passionate. It's so well connected in general to how we get students to think and be self-motivated and have internal drive.

One could argue that makerspaces are going the way of MOOCs[19]— only reinforcing the privilege and access of middle-class paradigms and still largely unused in lower-income, marginalized communities. If we really believe that makerspaces improve creativity, critical thinking, and STEM, what will it take for the movement to reach a more diverse audience?

Why I see the maker movement as being fundamentally different, is that I see it as hitting on different things, namely on student motivation and constructivist

---

[19] MOOC: Massive Open Online Course. Typically free for anyone who can access it.

education, with what we know about how students learn best, project-based instruction, and the evolution of progressive education. At the UTeach conference last May, we had several sessions about making in the classroom. It's important for us to embed this into regular coursework. Right now, a lot of the robotics and electives are afterschool activities, but in order for this to be truly democratized, we have to make it part of our classes — science and math that every kid takes. Next Generation Science Standards (NGSS) and Common Core State Standards (CCSS) math standards demonstrate value for persistent problem solvers, design cycle, and implementing inquiry. Makerspaces can support these standards for all students.

As part of the maker strand at our UTeach conference, Leah Buechley gave the plenary talk contrasting mainstream maker approaches with tools and techniques designed to support diversity and equality. This is exactly why we, in education, need to systematically develop opportunities around "making" for a more diverse population, which early indications show is working. We're already seeing that the demographics of youth-serving makerspaces are much more diverse than that of Maker Faire.

MIKE'S ONE GOOD QUESTION: How can we use makerspaces to address community needs? What we're doing is making things, but why are we making them?

ONE GOOD QUESTION WITH DR. MICHAEL GOETZ: HOW SCHOOL SPENDING IMPACTS CHANGE (USA)

Spending a lot of time with finance and economic experts can be intimidating for me, but one good question provided me with the cover that I needed to be intensely curious in this conversation. I had known Michael Goetz for years, but this was our first conversation about his area of expertise. While I had led a network of schools and could discuss the practicalities of school budget decisions and implications, Dr. Goetz specialized in analyzing fiscal data to develop models for PK-12 school finance equity and adequacy. As an education entrepreneur, none of my innovative ideas were about how we allocated our funding.

If I could go back in time, I would have had this interview before building our school model. I spent three years researching best practices for our instructional and staffing model, but it never occurred to me to research finance implications, finance equity, or simply put, which student interventions had a financially proven return on the investment. We cycled through several instructional intervention models before identifying the best model for our elementary school students. If you are developing a new school or supporting new school, district, or charter management leaders, start a conversation now about how education finance research could inform instructional innovation. If you are building a school governance or advisory board, recruit an education economist to help guide conversations about research-informed practice.

In what ways do our investments in education reveal our beliefs about the next generation's role in the world?

The biggest myth is that education can cure all social ills. Given the diversity of the population, it's not possible to equalize outcomes when the inputs are so different. That said, I think it's the greatest goal of the education system and should in fact be promoted with new effort. Therefore, school districts and states and the federal government should continue to close gaps based on socioeconomic class, as well as the conscious and unconscious racism and sexism inherent in our culture.

Happily, those programmatic strategies that help all children learn have the greatest effect on those struggling to learn, including the disenfranchised youth. That's why a focus on embedded intensive teacher professional development, tutoring, and other extra-help strategies for struggling students, and early interventions, such as quality Pre-K programs, should top the lists in most schools. These programs have shown the most impact on academic growth.

For decades, the US education funding system has been designed to ameliorate the academic and social inequalities produced by our economic and cultural disparities. Our federal, state, and local funding systems all contribute to priority in different ways. Federal funding, such as Headstart and Title I, and state/local funding formulas are designed to subsidize needs of low-income and/or marginalized groups. Despite their design, these funds don't necessarily perform in the ways that the public assumes. For example, the formula built for Title I funds includes a geographical sparsity index, which means that more funds per student may go to Wyoming than to inner city LA. There is a similar disparity with state financing that links to property wealth. State formula funds are allocated to counteract the property wealth of local municipalities. In the 1980s, states began spending more money on education than local governments. Since states were "purchasing" education at a higher rate, they felt more entitled to have a say about what happens in schools. Essentially, these funding inequities compelled states to introduce standards-based movements. Standards and accountability-based movements at the federal level show disparities between and within states as well as between and within districts and schools.

Often, we use our preconceived notions about education outcomes to inform our decisions. What are the biggest myths about how education works in the US that we continue to fund?

What could be possible for education outcomes if we shifted our funding away from X and did Y instead? The other big myth is that the sheer existence of additional funds can help cure education shortcomings. School finance experts debate all the time whether more money matters. But all of us agree that how money is used matters. For example, in every economics research study, I ask a group of teacher leaders what they need to bring struggling students up to par. The answer is always an additional program and it's always 20% more funding than they currently receive. We have returned to the same community after a decade of the program implementation, and they ask for another 20% budget increase! What happens is that they take the new funds and use them to reinforce existing programs and services instead of restructuring their expenditures.

They supplement versus supplant? Yes, you're on the right track. What they're doing is taking the money and applying it to things that they already do. When a school or district's programs are not producing results, more of the same does not lead to improvement; redistribution of current resources and infusing new, evidence-based programming is the smarter decision.

So what should schools ask for? Most educators and education lobbyists approach funding requests from a loss mindset: we have endured budget cuts and we want you to restore our full funding. When educators understand what achievement students will make as a direct result of the new program, then they can make need-based asks: if awarded an extra $4,000, I will be able to graduate one more student, because that's the proven result of the XYZ program.

Statistically, we know many programs, when implemented well, impact student achievement for all students, such as intensive embedded teacher professional development, which requires full-time instructional coaching, and introduction of certified teachers as tutors. Those are two of the most effective strategies and the hardest ones to implement with fidelity. What education economists will tell you is that if you don't mandate implementation, you likely will not see positive academic outcomes because resources will be used for the existing programming. We suggest that states start without any mandates and then look at the schools that are not performing well. If they haven't implemented these strategies yet, then start slowly mandating the interventions — start with instructional coaches in year one, then maybe certified tutors in year two.

What should districts and schools stop funding? This is highly controversial, but what continues to elude me is how many facets of life in which the schooling system attempts to take part. Schooling should be good at educating students to standards. This is their priority. Rhetorically, "why are schools in the business of transportation, food service, security, medical care, and athletics ?" I'm not saying that these are not useful periphery services to academics, but I do suggest schools should focus on what they do best: educate students. These periphery services may take place on campus, but I question whether the education system should be directly responsible. I do not expect superintendents to lay concrete at the new school, but I do expect the superintendent to contract out this service to a reputable company that actually has experience laying concrete. This is what people would be calling community involvement in education. Struggling schools should cut out all athletics from their school and move to community-based sports teams. This will increase community involvement for athletics and be aligned with international practices. Economically, it may create a surplus to fund necessary academic interventions, or it may not. However, it would allow schools to get on with educating students.

> **MICHAEL'S ONE GOOD QUESTION:** How much input should local, state, and federal governments have on the programmatic strategies of schools, given their variation in education goals and knowledge of effective programs?

ONE GOOD QUESTION WITH NICOLE DE BEAUFORT: WHAT IF WE BUILT EDUCATION FUNDING ON ABUNDANCE, NOT SCARCITY? (USA)

In the next two interviews, I speak with Nicole de Beaufort and Dan Varner. As a result of interviewing them separately, I learned that they had actually worked together in Detroit! I met Nicole and Dan under completely different circumstances, and it didn't occur to me that their work was interrelated. In retrospect, it makes sense, and in some ways, these two conversations felt like one long interview. At the time of our conversation, Nicole was most focused on early childhood access and the intersecting needs of families living below the federal poverty line. Dan was still the Executive Director of Excellent Schools Detroit and while we spoke mostly about that work, his one good question brought us back to early childhood education.

In what ways do our investments in education reveal our beliefs about the next generation's role in the world?

I try to look at this question through multiple lenses, those of foundations, government, and direct services, as well as that of the ultimate end user — families. Ultimately, I want to know how well people are informing stakeholders about problems and solutions. In Detroit, much of my work is in early childhood. I often hear early childhood practitioners ask: Why are we always just at minimum? Why is funding minimum? What would happen if we built formulas for the abundance, not the scarcity? We're always working on minimums of state and federal funding and that has a negative effect on the system.

When we mold to the minimum, we're building for somebody else's kids. It's discrimination against poor people. When an early education professional with two master's degrees makes $10 to $12 per hour, the system is broken. When every month or quarter early childhood centers have to justify their existence and they have already stretched every dollar, the system is broken. We have normalized these low investments and expect people to make miracles happen for the next generation without sufficient capacity.

What would change things?

1. Universal Pre-K that's not defined by your ZIP code. No matter who you are or where you live, you should get the same education.
2. Pay equity. Early childhood educators are barely paid more than fast food workers. We can't deliver high-quality universal Pre-K until we start respecting our educators.
3. Remove institutional barriers to early childhood access. Models like half-day Pre-K are false choices for low-income families. In places like Detroit, where there's not much transit or cars, there are structural barriers to such models. It takes ninety minutes to drop your kids off, and if you're a few minutes late, your child is turned away and you have to take them home on the same ninety-minute bus ride. At some point parents decide that it's not worth the trouble.
4. Make parent involvement about partnership, not compliance. The lack of transit infrastructure is compounded by punitive compliance-driven practices at the school level. Successful universal Pre-K will have parent engagement goals that are relevant and focused on developmental supports for their children.

Earlier in our conversation you said that it takes at least ten years for structural change to happen. What do the next ten years of this work look like in Michigan?

In the beginning, we should focus on state and local partnerships. We would engage in common visioning and develop a common understanding of the realities of local, state, and federal funding streams. The Citizens Research Council of Michigan publishes a catalogue with the type of data that creates space for decision-makers to identify our strengths, our capacity, and our inadequacies. For example, a recent IFF study shows the gap between the available quality seats in early childhood education and the kids in need. The highest need goes in a band around the city and into the suburbs. If we were all reviewing that information, we would see that this is not a Detroit problem, it's a regional problem.

Once there's a shared understanding of where to go (vision) and why (purpose), then you can tackle the question: How do you turn a regional issue into a workable issue? For example, with their Science and Cultural Facilities District, Denver created a tax which enabled some regional thinking about the solutions. A proposal like that could be helpful for building a regional conversation on early childhood. At present, Dearborn and Detroit don't think that they have the same problems.

Finally, focus on impact metrics: How will we know that universal early childhood is working?

1. When we see parent demand for quality early childhood rise.
2. When quality early childhood programs don't have empty seats.
3. When you have robust public conversation about quality of life for parents with young kids.
4. When the conversation is actively about learning, no longer bemoaning the fact that we don't have good options.
5. Once the focus is more on the nuance of what/how our children are learning and less on how the institution is performing, we'll know that we've achieved universal access of acceptable quality for all families.

> **NICOLE'S ONE GOOD QUESTION:** How do we create cities and communities where we don't have decisions made solely on economic terms? How do we address the divide between the Dollar Store community and the Amazon community?

ONE GOOD QUESTION WITH DAN VARNER: IS GENDER BIAS KEEPING THE US FROM INVESTING IN PRE-K? (USA)

In what ways do our investments in education reveal our beliefs about the next generation's role in the world?

What do we believe the purpose of education is? I've come to the conclusion that there is no singular answer. I don't think our society holds a single answer. One of the reasons that education is as contested a subject as it is, is because the answer to this question is different for different people. Education is one of the few places where we actually tax ourselves as a community and contribute funds willingly for some perceived greater good. Our investment in education reveals one thing: the next generation has such a significant and important role to play in the world, that it is worthwhile for us to invest in them as kids in order to prepare them for that.

Secondly, education is necessary to help folks govern themselves more effectively. How democratic is our democracy? Education has always been important to access that franchise effectively and stay informed about the political process. We believe in the next generation's role in governing itself and us as a community. I won't take it too far because we don't actually invest in citizenship classes/government; that's not where we end up targeting our education investments, but the notion is that a well-educated public governs effectively.

We see the increasing notion over the last century that we educate people to help them get better jobs. When factories and line jobs were the standard, education was a system that prepared those workers — cohorts that moved along the factory floor together; it did not prepare students in large numbers for inquiry and critical thinking. Emergence of old-style career and vocational education over the last sixty to seventy years is proof of that as well.

There is a small and growing movement around 21st century skills — deeper learning folks, Common Core State Standards (CCSS) — who believe that what's actually important are critical thinking skills, collaboration, and teamwork. Increasingly there are investments that reveal our belief in the importance of those things in comparison.

The US is unique in the way that we invest in early childhood and post-secondary education. Our historically high level of investment in post-secondary education reveals a fundamental belief in the value of thought — critical thinking, liberal arts, renaissance thinkers. In contrast to the investments in our K-12 system, however, I don't think our investments in post-secondary education reflects so much the belief about the next generation, but rather the current generation. We do a remarkably bad job at investing in early childhood education. We have evidenced a fundamental misunderstanding about the role of early childhood, and I suspect that is driven by a misbelief about the role of women in the current generation and their role as primary care providers and caregivers, and not as educators. It's a huge miss and a huge failure on our part.

I focus on how we move from where we are to where we want to be. In the early childhood discourse, I don't hear people refer to the social reasons and the perceived role of women in the workforce that contribute to low investments in early childhood education. Women in the workforce is a fairly new phenomenon in our country. For centuries, we assumed that women would care for their young children. There was a gender bias associated with childcare. If childcare had been the role of men, countries would have changed a long time ago to give male lawyers paternity breaks and years of pay. Our social and gender stereotypes and norms have influenced policy. It wasn't until the 1960s that we started HeadStart. That had something to do with our lack of any real belief in equitable treatment of folks, regardless of economic status and race. I suspect it's a combination of all of these beliefs and biases that have gotten us to where we are.

The creation of Excellent Schools Detroit marked a significant mindset shift into seeing the success of all students, regardless of school format, as the responsibility of the full community. What are your early lessons and how can other communities replicate/improve upon a similar investment in PreK-12?

1. You need a broad coalition of stakeholders, and they have to be in it for the long haul if you're going to win the effort or redefine the paradigm. There are

a whole set of stakeholders who are vested in the current system, regardless of outcomes. They are on the right and left and run the political gamut.

2. Governance matters AND, more importantly, governance can only hope to solve a small subset of the challenges that need to be resolved. Our experience in Detroit that led to the creation of the coalition is that we have low and high performing district and charter schools. Yes, governance can play a role in all of it, but it's not the magic bullet. In the whole picture, success matters more than the governance model.

3. Recognize that these are community challenges, not school challenges. The solutions we need are all around us. My favorite movie inspirational scene is Al Pacino's locker room speech in [the movie] *Any Given Sunday.* "A step too soon or a step too early and you miss your block, the inches we need are all around us." The creation of our coalition was a recognition that the inches we need are all around us — we need them in schools and green space and food and healthcare and the whole network of services that matters.

Recognize the multiple and competing purposes for which education exists.

4. We knew that we wanted a scorecard that measured the performance of schools and Michigan didn't do that. Parents would be faced with lots of data to understand their choices and we need to enable parents to make those choices. Test data told us something, but scores weren't the only data point — academic data only tells a small sliver of the whole story. We wanted to try to capture information to tell some of the larger story for folks. To do that, we needed closer partnership between community and schools. So we organized unannounced community site visits to schools based on the criteria that matters to the community. Part of that model is to help school leaders understand that they're ultimately accountable to the community, parents, and kids. These visits created a bridge for the community. Education can be pretty opaque for the average person, so this was an effort to help the community increase their understanding of what's going on in school buildings.

What advice would you give to a new community who says, "Let's start doing pop-up school site visits !"

Schools loved it, both in theory and in practice. Schools knew that they weren't performing well on the standardized test, so this was one way to showcase their other value-adds that tell additional stories of school success. That was the theoretical buy in. Then in practice, schools were pleased with our process. Schools had to opt in to the process (86% participated), and we promised that, for the first year of visits, none of the data would be public or real-time. We trained community members on how to walk through a school building during the day. Schools have now figured out that they need to get parents to walk through their buildings, especially for enrollment in the transition years. Our biggest lesson from the school visits? The site visit data was not strongly correlated to standardized test data. As a result, it's hard to fund the site visit model.

DAN'S ONE GOOD QUESTION: Why do we assume, like in the traditional cohort model, that all kids should start school at the same age?

ONE GOOD QUESTION WITH KATHY PADIAN: HOW DOES LEADERSHIP TRUMP FUNDING IN SCHOOL SYSTEM IMPROVEMENT? (USA)

The first year that I was researching and writing the blog series, I was also exploring where in the country our family might move. Every time I took a work trip, I looked at that city as a potential home and assessed housing options, school options, and our network of family and friends. New Orleans was high on the list with my family as the biggest draw, but I had not worked in New Orleans since I was 18. When I discussed potentially moving home to Adrian Morgan, a friend and fellow educator in New Orleans, he suggested that I meet with his partner to get the lay of the land in the post-Katrina education community.

I first met Kathy Padian over dinner at Luke in the Central Business District. Sidenote: get the Luke burger, it changed my life. Adrian and Kathy were among the cohort of national education leaders who had come to the city in the years following Hurricane Katrina recovery. Kathy had led strategic education, facilities, and development work in Washington D.C. and New York before coming to New Orleans and eventually became Deputy Superintendent of Orleans Parish School Board, our local district. Kathy had unique perspectives on how the district rebuilt itself and whether any of the structural changes could or should be replicated in other traditional school districts.

In what ways do our investments in education reveal our beliefs about the next generation's role in the world?

The first thing that comes to mind is the disparity among different communities and their investments. In a recent meeting about school turnaround, we learned about Camden, NJ, where they spend $26,000 per student in a district with 15,000 students. The majority of us in the room, our heads exploded. Here we are, in a very impoverished state and city where housing prices are rising and we're still investing around $10,000 per student. It's mind boggling. When I read that question, I was thinking overall in the US, we don't invest nearly enough. Kids should have the ability to go to a classroom or education environment from birth or two to three years-old if they want to (not mandatory). In Louisiana we don't require school until seven, which is a crazy law. There needs to be a much greater investment. We hear all the sound bites about a different type of future and technology-based innovation entrepreneurial thinkers etc., yet in many places (not Camden), we are falling woefully short on the investment side, and education becomes the easiest thing to cut from a budget (especially early childhood education). We're not putting our money where our mouth is. The national defense budget is quadrupling in comparison to education.

In the post-Katrina New Orleans education landscape, we've seen considerable economic resources invested in outcomes for youth. Which ones have had the greatest game-changing impact? Which investments are replicable for other underperforming urban school communities?

From where I sit, the greatest game-changing impact wasn't specifically economic. There was no money that changed things. It was more the ability to restart. In pre-Katrina New Orleans, if you were able to, you sent your kids to private or parochial schools. If you were not able to, there was some relationship between not having the money for private school and lack of grassroots agency to create change. Pre-Katrina, there were absolutely small pockets of schools and folks who were trying to do things differently, but the mentality was, "I can't save everyone, so I'm going to save this subset of kids." It seemed so intractable.

Getting to where you remove the massive money suck at the central office, is probably the thing that was the game changer. I don't know how other cities can replicate that. Does state takeover create that space? Outsiders think that New Orleans education recovery was flooded with funding, but the funding was targeted. New Orleans received a federal investment and FEMA support to rebuild school buildings. Like everything in Louisiana, we didn't hire the right people. We had people with no experience who were hired to manage billion-dollar budgets. The money wasn't managed better, however, or we could have had more buildings or better status for the construction.

So what can make the central office different? You need a mix of veteran and newcomer administrators. This is one of the five recommendations in The Wallace Foundation's brief on the role of district leadership in school improvement. In any existing administration, there are good and hardworking team members who, if they had good leadership with visionary direction, would adapt and be great. You also need people who are coming from the outside (of the district or region) and who have seen different ways of doing things. These two cohorts need to work alongside each other. You need that mix: outsiders who come in with some humility and are willing to work with veterans and veterans who want to adapt. Building and guiding such a team requires really strong leadership to get everyone on the same team and working towards the same goal.

The Recovery School District[20] was getting there, but now the pendulum has swung the other way. We currently have a super young team with lots of energy, who are now starting to try "new ideas" that, in some cases, were the same old ideas from before. Old heads hear these "new ideas" and are loath to work with the new staffers. This is maddening because there was an opportunity for Orleans Parish to bring the schools back. The bridge building that we began could have continued — to bring the fresh ideas and the institutional knowledge together in the same place. But that's not happening, and with the new governor, who knows how the legislature will respond? We're not ready for change, but politics may force the hand.

> **KATHY'S ONE GOOD QUESTION:** Why aren't there more women superintendents and leaders of large Charter Management Organizations (CMOs)?

---

[20] Recovery School District in Louisiana is a state-wide agency created in 2003 to support the state's lowest performing schools. Several states in the US have similar state-run districts called Achievement School Districts.

WHAT ARE YOU WONDERING?

MIKE WONDERS: How can we use this space to address community needs? What we're doing is making things, but why are we making them?

MICHAEL WONDERS: How much input should local, state, and federal governments have on the programmatic strategies of schools, given their variation in education goals and knowledge of effective programs?

NICOLE WONDERS: How do we create cities and communities where we don't have decisions made solely on economic terms? How do we address the divide between the Dollar Store community and the Amazon community?

DAN WONDERS: Why do we assume, like in the traditional cohort model, that all kids should start school at the same age?

KATHY WONDERS: Why aren't there more women superintendents and leaders of large Charter Management Organizations (CMOs)?

When you think about funding for public education, at the local, state, or federal level, what comes to mind? What did you already know about education funding that was challenged here?

As you reflect on your one good question —

- Think about your audience: Which voices were missing from this chapter? Who are the experts for your wondering?
- Think about your context: What considerations for education funding would matter most for your local needs?
- Think about your timing: Are you trying to get clarity on what has occurred or on what could be?

7 BOOKS, 2 TALKS, 1 TV SHOW AND AL PACINO – WHAT ONE GOOD QUESTION FOLKS ARE READING.

During every *One Good Question* interview, we had awesome side conversations and anecdotes that did not make the final edit. I noticed that my reading list grew in direct relationship to our sidebars. As you start planning your personal syllabus, here are a few titles that may resonate with you:

On design
Aylon Samouha: *The End of Average: How We Succeed in a World That Values Sameness*, Todd Rose (2016)

Rose opens his TED Talk and book with the following poignant anecdote. "In the 1940s as planes were getting faster and more complex, there was a spike in plane crashes. They checked the planes and said the planes were fine, but the pilots were making errors. They tried to solve for the pilot errors and began designing the cockpit for 'the average pilot.' They took some average pilot demographics and sized to adjust, but there were still no improvements in performance. They quickly learned that none of the 400 pilots sampled actually measured the average size of their calculations. The cockpit wasn't designed for any real person. Eventually they tried to fit the system to the individual and invented adjustable seats, etc., things that we take for granted now." In the book. you learn that's the secret of all design: "Any system that is trying to fit the individual is actually doomed to fail."

On elite education
Peter Howe: *Excellent Sheep*, William Deresiewicz (2014)

Deresiewicz is a first-generation immigrant whose father was a professor. His basic premise is that elite education in the US is producing intellectual sheep who are terrified of failure. These youth grow up with model CVs from birth, but have no resilience, creativity or desire to think outside of the box.

Without giving it all away, he concludes that, "If we are here to create a decent society, a just society, a wise and prosperous society, a society where children can learn for the love of learning and people can work for the love of work...We don't have to love our neighbors as ourselves, but we need to love our neighbors' children as our own...We have tried aristocracy, we have tried meritocracy, now it's time to try democracy."

On local funding
Susanna Williams: *Parks and Recreation*, NBC (2009 - 2015)

When it comes to political engagement, we tend to focus on national policy and the influence of national lobby groups. The general public has little understanding about how state and local funding decisions are made. State government deals with the important daily stuff, but it's not sexy, so there's a lack of TV/entertainment exposure to those decisions. If you want to learn about local funding issues, watch the TV show *Parks and Recreation*. In most states, local legislature is limited to those whose jobs allow them to have flexible jobs for six months — ranchers and farmers in western states and self-funded individuals who are so wealthy that they don't need to work. That's who's making our local policy and funding decisions.

On creating coalitions
Dan Varner: *Any Given Sunday*, Oliver Stone (1999)

My favorite inspirational movie scene is a great speech from *Any Given Sunday*. Al Pacino's in the locker room and giving his football team the encouragement to get back out and turn the game around. "The inches we need are everywhere around us. On this team, we fight for that inch." His point, and the way that it inspires me, is that when creating our coalition, we had to recognize that "the inches we needed" were already there — in our schools, green space, food service, healthcare — and it was up to us to harness that power.

On diversity in ed tech
Mike DeGraff: "Making Good: Equality and Diversity in Maker Education,"
Leah Buechley (2015)

In Leah's talk, she highlights the imperative we have to define maker education separately from the mainstream Maker Magazine and Faires. Those events tend to be homogenous groups that reflect the values and interests of its audience. To me, this is exactly why we, in education, need to systematically develop opportunities around making for a more diverse population, which, early indications show, is working.

On questioning
Anu Passi-Rauste: *A More Beautiful Question: The Power of Inquiry to Spark Breakthrough Ideas*, **Warren Berger (2014)**

I was visiting a small nonprofit in Boston and the ED recommended this book to me. It's all about how to make a good question. My one big takeaway is that I need to figure out my one good question before I start my next project. What is the most beautiful question that I want to raise?

On accountability
Tony Monfiletto: *The Allure of Order: High Hopes, Dashed Expectations, and the Troubled Quest to Remake American Schooling*, **Jal Mehta (2013)**

Mehta outlines how the investment in accountability at the back end of the education system is an effort to make up for the fact that we haven't invested as aggressively in the front end. We don't put enough time, energy, or strategy into good school design, preparation of teachers, or capital development. Because we don't put enough resources into those areas, we try to make up for it in accountability structures.

On solving complex problems
Tom Vander Ark: *The Ingenuity Gap: How Can We Solve the Problems of the Future?*, Thomas Homer-Dixon (2010)

Dixon's work centers on the fact that we seem incapable of addressing our basic problems. The problems that we're facing in society grow in complexity. Their interrelatedness with each other and our civic problem-solving capacity is diminishing. We've created enormously complex systems, but we have more and more black swan events that we can't predict or solve. If you're trying to figure out how to address complex system needs, this book helps to order your thinking.

On AI
Tom Vander Ark: *The Singularity is Near: When Humans Transcend Biology*, Ray Kurzweil (2005)

People have a linear memory and we assume that the future will be like the past, but the future is happening exponentially faster than we appreciate. In *The Singularity is Near*, Kurzweil posits that computers will be smarter than people, and while we know it's happening, we can't fully understand the implications of that trajectory.

On bias
Rhonda Broussard: *Blindspot: Hidden Biases of Good People*, Mahzarin Banaji & Anthony Greenwald (2013)

This is the psychology behind the Project Implicit research and it's fascinating. Through clever analogies, card tricks, and pop culture references, the researchers teach us how our brains create bias, how that can convert to prejudice or discrimination, and how to make peace when our aspirational beliefs and implicit biases are at odds.

WHO BENEFITS FROM SCHOOL REDESIGN EFFORTS?

CHAPTER 4

IN 2015, it seemed like every recovering education administrator had a bold vision for a new school model. Everyone told the same Rip Van Winkle story to emphasize why we needed a departure from the industrial school model — we were still operating school on an agrarian calendar and reinforcing habits of the manufacturing floor. In my own school design, we tinkered around the edges — slightly longer school year, deeper professional development, shared voice, shared power practices with families — but all within the confines of the traditional school building and the traditional school day. One of the unintended byproducts of navigating COVID-19 in 2020 is that it forced every education leader in the world to make unforeseen shifts in their practice, and to implement these shifts at scale.

Just as I was wrapping up the blog interview series, I had an opportunity to meet two new school founders: Kimberly Neal-Brannum and Stefin Pasternak were both developing new high school models in Indianapolis and New Orleans respectively. When we met, they were in two different school design fellowships that afforded them two to three years to build their school model. Living School opened in New Orleans in August 2019 with forty students in ninth grade. Believe Schools welcomed their first ninth graders in August 2020, right in the middle of the pandemic. Before we revisit pre-COVID ideas for school redesign, let's take a look at how redesign manifested within the constraints of a global health pandemic.

Believe Schools - Indianapolis, Indiana

I met Kimberly Neal-Brannum in 2016 when she was designing Believe Schools, a network of high-performing high schools that centered the needs of Black and Brown youth. Neal-Brannum was not a newcomer to school start-up work. She had led high school start-up and turnaround for charter management organizations like Noble Schools in Chicago and KIPP in Washington, D.C.

> "After six years of college, our college completion averages were 40%. Kids were not completing college, then [they were] coming home with no transitional skills and working at the airport. It felt like a loss, and it inspired me to push the Believe Schools model to set our students up for success post-Believe. I can't control the college environment, the family environment, or their finances to get them to graduate. We focus on our students' first careers; that's how we frame it."
>
> - Kimberly Neal-Brannum

When she designed the network, she originally envisioned that all students would earn Associates' degrees and/or professional certificates along with their high school diploma. She was planning to have customized course pathways with local university partners to make this a reality. A self-described traditionalist before COVID-19, Neal-Brannum believed that kids learned better with pen and paper, book in hand, and stand and deliver instruction. When she thought about computers in the classroom, she always saw them as a supplement to teacher instruction, not as a replacement for them.

Believe Circle City High School, their first campus in Indianapolis, IN, opened in the fall of 2020 to in-person, socially distanced instruction. When asked how COVID-19 impacted the school model, Neal-Brannum notes that "The pandemic has forced us to be creative. I hope that creativity will live long past the pandemic."

An unexpected benefit of the COVID education constraints was for students with chronic absenteeism. Black and Brown youth in lower income communities often have higher family care responsibilities than their middle-class peers. They may miss days of school in order to care for younger siblings, aging grandparents, and adults with elevated health needs. Recent immigrants will often travel home for a month to see their families and, as a result, students would miss that much instructional time. Believe Schools, like most schools in Indianapolis, has been providing in-person instruction since August 2020. At a time when their peer schools with in-person instruction were not supporting distance learning, Believe Schools issued devices to all students and created flexible, hybrid instruction. As a result, those students with higher family care responsibilities didn't lose instructional time. The students who went to the Dominican Republic with their family for a month still had access to school and could remain involved in their instruction and educational community. Neal-Brannum notes that trust is the most important factor with virtual instruction. "To some extent, by allowing our students to take devices home, we may be evening out the playing field in our school."

In response to COVID restrictions, Neal-Brannum fast-tracked the use of technology to replace direct instruction in two of their six courses — biology and composition. She was never an advocate for blended learning models and says that the courses were met with mixed results — some students thrived with online instruction and others less so. Early indicators were that course content like biology was more straightforward, whereas an online course for composition was more challenging for budding writers. Like every data-driven leader, Neal-Brannum wanted to wait to see how her students performed on the interim assessments before making a decision about whether or not to keep the online courses for the following year. The questions that she's asking of the data and her school model are still about possibility. How well are students able to apply their learning from online courses? If students perform well on their state assessment with only online instruction, could that become a viable option for standard level courses? A breakthrough like that would allow Neal-Brannum to help students develop a highly customized high school diploma, reserving live, in-person instruction for the courses that are most aligned with each student's post-secondary path. "I hope that, post-pandemic, we can partner with outside entities to allow our students to maximize their learning based on their passions and not be funneled into one system where everyone gets the same things."

Living School - New Orleans, Louisiana

In New Orleans, there's so little variation in our seasons that it can be hard to remember what time of the year something happened solely based on the weather. That explains why I can't quite recall when I had my first real conversation with Stefin Pasternak. I know that we met in City Park and walked the short picturesque loop around the lake and the longer, less manicured loop around the Festival Grounds. We spent much of that walk talking about what led to our realizations about our work and vision for the role of formal education in liberation movements.

Pasternak traces his inspiration for Living School back to his time as a sixth grade writing teacher at the top performing open enrollment school in New Orleans. In 2010, the city was commemorating the five-year anniversary of Hurricane Katrina and every education reform zealot was looking for proof points of the new possible. Pasternak's school, and his classroom, was seen as one of those bright spots.

> "Every other month, the doors of my classroom would burst open with a different billionaire who would enthusiastically proclaim, 'What you guys are doing is amazing, we want to replicate this everywhere!' The CMO would get an influx of cash and the network proliferated. The next wave to visit was educators who wanted to come and learn our secret sauce so they could replicate our practices."
>
> - Stefin Pasternak

The accolades didn't sit well with Pasternak and his peers. They didn't think that they had developed anything worth emulating and it sparked an inquiry for them about what they really believed about teaching and learning. In 2012, a group of faculty, families, and students started organizing around this question and named five ways that structural racism and oppression manifested in their work:

1. They were teaching the wrong things. Education was reduced to literacy and numeracy, and they thought learning should be broader.
2. They were teaching in the wrong ways. The overemphasis on standardized testing would not lead young people to live liberated lives. How could pedagogy honor youth capabilities and let them do real-world work now?
3. They saw current education systems as a metaphor for intentionally segregated and monocrop farming communities. In an industrial agriculture model, we measure success by yield of corn per acre. It looks like they're doing amazing things — we've increased our yield. But if you zoom out and look at the quality of the soil and nutrition for humans, they're both devastating. Test scores were that crop. They zoomed out and looked at the impact of those

test scores; our students' experiences were still devastated. They wanted to build intentional biodiversity and think about school as an ecosystem. Our students, staff, families, and parents were diverse, and they deserved diverse teaching methods. They envisioned a school that would name some best practices and norms and let everyone riff on them creatively.

4. There was no vested power for all of the stakeholders. When it was time for decision making that impacted students and parents, they were never at the table.

5. They were measuring the wrong things. Like most schools, their primary metrics were student test scores and how often students misbehaved. That approach led to better test scores and more misbehaving.

After years of organizing, designing with their community, and studying different schools and societies with more democratic practices, Living School welcomed their first class of ninth graders in August 2019. That spring, like the rest of the schools in the country, the school made emergency plans for distance learning and family support. Many Living School families struggled with COVID-related unemployment. The Board of Directors approved funding for care packages and targeted assistance for families in the most dire crisis, and the school delivered these throughout the summer.

Living School was able to be very nimble in their COVID response, something that Pasternak attributes to both their size and tenure. As a first-year school, on some level their community expected them to still be figuring everything out. They leveraged their school's democratic structure to adjust to the real-time evolving circumstances in the pandemic.

> "We crafted the policy with all three stakeholder groups — student council is our legislative branch, staff council is executive, family council is judicial. We decided when to go along with our local district, and when to break from the district because of the unique needs and circumstances of our community. One example of that was the decision we made in the third quarter. The winter spike in COVID cases was happening and the district was changing their metrics and making decisions pretty last-minute. Our councils got ahead of the situation and made a decision that would best serve us. We voted to stay all virtual in the third quarter and then revisit [in-person options] for the fourth quarter."

When asked which COVID-inspired shifts they might keep in the future, Pasternak said the jury was still out on that, but there were three positive outcomes that they had not anticipated. Because students were not in the building, there were fewer disciplinary challenges, which in turn led to a stronger focus on learning. Compared to when a student takes a break from a traditional school setting, which makes them lose instructional time, virtual instruction meant that even with disciplinary consequences, students didn't have to lose any instructional access. Finally, managing home and family care is a pervasive need for educators, but COVID offered a new range of accommodations for adults as well. For the educators who could manage digital engagement, they've experienced more work/life balance than before.

What's one traditional education concept that Pasternak hopes will be debunked as a result of COVID? Instructional minutes. How can state departments of education redefine what counts as required instructional minutes to pass a class?

> **STEFIN'S ONE GOOD QUESTION:** What would it look like to prioritize health and wellbeing over economy? What is the relationship between the two?

In this chapter we hear from: Tom Vander Ark (USA) on the relationship between school redesign and education equity. Connie K. Chung (USA) explores the need for transparency about best practices. Tony Monfiletto (USA) challenges whether we have the right people engaged in school redesign. Saku Tuominen (Finland) questions the twentieth century success of the Finnish education model. Noelle Lim (Malaysia) wonders how to inspire communities to look beyond standardized tests. Anna Hall (USA) breaks down the school redesign process and the questions she encourages along the way. Aylon Samouha (USA) wonders how we can get research-based practices in the hands of educators faster.

ONE GOOD QUESTION WITH ANNA HALL: CAN YOU BREAK UP WITH YOUR BEST IDEAS? (USA)

Once I started publishing the "One Good Question" blog, educators around the globe took notice. I had never heard of Springpoint: Partners in School Design before, but after reading one of my blog posts, they contacted me via Twitter to inquire about doing an interview for One Good Question.

That's how I officially met Anna Hall, but if you ask me about her work, I always picture the day that we spent visiting one of their partner schools in Manhattan. A month or so after our interview, I was in New York for a project and met up with Anna and a colleague at a pastry shop in the Financial District. We walked over to one of their school design partners, The Urban Assembly Maker Academy (Murry Bergtraum Campus). We did the typical school site visit routine: met with an administrator to get the big vision for the school, visited a few classes in action, and talked to students about their experiences. This campus of Urban Assembly is a CTE school within the New York City Department of Education which means it prepares all students for a career and technical education. While there were parts of their school model that I found intriguing, what struck me most was its continuous iteration of their model. Before this visit, I thought of school design support as a discrete phase of start-up school development, not as a long-term strategic support. In this interview, Anna Hall explores how longer school design cycles can bring more students into the process.

In what ways do our investments in education reveal our beliefs about the next generation's role in the world?

Our field is collectively investing in new school development and engines that can generate new designs for school. Those two things sometimes happen simultaneously and sometimes run on parallel tracks. In the new school development work, there are districts and cities around the country that have invested very heavily in opening new schools to change the paradigm for what high schools could be — NYC, DC, and NOLA come to mind. Deeply embedded in that investment is a commitment to equity and choice; as a system, we are committed to creating great opportunities for young people and ensuring that they and their families have a range of choices for where they want to go. That's urgent, exciting work.

But in addition to offering more great high schools, we know that we also need to make sure that we have evolved high schools with designs that advance as quickly as the world we live in. It's important to acknowledge that creating a truly world class system of twenty-first-century-ready schools will require a multitude of design solutions or models. It's inspiring, however, to be able to work simultaneously in new school design efforts that focus on that challenge.

Why does equity matter in school design?

Learning is part of becoming a fully formed, socially and culturally engaged human. We all have a right to do it, and our society has a responsibility to create those learning opportunities. All kids should have a chance to go to a great school, designed to support them and give them opportunities to shine. I started teaching, in fact, because in my twenties I worked for a child welfare agency whose stated chief academic goal for the young people in its care was that they achieved their GED. I was deeply disturbed by the inequity and unfairness of that premise, by the idea that our system would organize around such low expectations for young people who had already navigated so much trauma and struggle in their lives. I knew kids could do more, given the right opportunity and support. I joined the NYC Teaching Fellows and have been an educator and a school designer ever since, because I believe we can and must create better systems, better schools, better choices and support for young people and their families.

When working with educators on school redesign, how do you narrate the new design process for them?

It depends. If you're working with a team attempting to open a new school but not a new model, that's an easier soup to dive into because things seem known. You're taking the core of someone else's practice and building a design around it. We recently published a collection of some of the questions and experiences from the design process that our partners have found most relevant and helpful — but to sum up here, we've found that the real challenge for completely new model design is actually reframing the task at hand — understanding that you are trying to create a custom-built school that maps to and builds upon your specific students' ambitions, dreams, strengths, and needs, not just curating a set of great ideas that could be engaging to any group of kids. And we recognize that "design" is work that school leaders and their teams may engage in as part of the process of creating a new concept for a school — that it continues in perpetuity after the school opens, as part of a robust iteration cycle.

> "Stop for a second. Look at the young people in your schools. Consider what path those young people need to get to where they want to go. Then build."
>
> - Anna Hall

Step 1: Breaking up

If you accept the premise that schools should be built uniquely to serve the students in them, then new school model design requires designers to begin the work without a preconception of what their school should be. In this context, designers don't have to be married to a certain schedule, or course sequence, or bells, lunch, etc. Instead, we encourage them to launch their design work by developing a deep understanding of the students and families their school will serve, and then build from there. This "frame-breaking" work can be challenging, but it can also be really creative and fun. It lets us think about how to organize school around what our kids need.

Step 2: Wow!

We have inspired the most beautiful design! Often, design teams come up with inspiring, innovative design concepts that look great on paper. But the act of translating the design into systems that work for faculty and all of the families and young people is often when folks hit the second wall. Again, we encourage design teams to look at their designs through the lens of student needs and assets and prioritize based on local context and realities.

Step 3: Oh crap!

This is often how teams react when they have to decide how to actually bring their designs to life. They have to answer many questions: In which order will we create and roll out each design element? Which people do we try to hire and recruit and who will be willing to do this? What is the enrollment pattern around our school and its ecosystem? How do we both navigate logistics and protect our model? It's an intellectual puzzle — arranging the pieces and putting everything in place. It can be a messy exercise.

Step 4: Euphoria

When schools open for the first time, and through the first few weeks, teams often feel like they're walking on air: "We made a thing! A real thing! People are here! Children are here! They're doing things that look like school. It's amazing!!!!!" It is really a lovely moment while it lasts.

Step 5: Breaking up (again)

Shortly thereafter, things start to break or not work. The ideas that were awesome might not fit because a team couldn't predict what their students would need or want or respond well to, or what might not work in practice. We help our partners navigate that first wave of struggle: My original ideas were not perfect, so what's the path forward? How do you break up with the parts of your idea that just don't fit your current reality? How do you deal with that emotionally? Then, practically speaking, because you have young people in the space and adults who are trying to do their job well — how do you make shifts strategically, without causing too much disruption and stress? Consistency is important: How do you maintain a baseline of quality for your kids that you can sustain, whatever your changes?

I love that students are your starting and ending point! How much do students participate in this process?

Our position is that we want students to participate fully and as much as possible in the process. When we started this work, our first school partners already knew which communities their new schools would serve and where their feeder schools were. This was a great opportunity, which meant teams wouldn't have to design in abstract — they could solve specific challenges. So as we developed our process, we saw that student knowledge as an asset, and we designed a process that capitalizes on that information.

Given that, as I mentioned before, we believe that every school design team needs to start with a deep immersion in the process of understanding the community and families and students that the new school will serve. Instead of starting with an academic model, we encourage designers to spend time talking to families and kids. What are their ambitions, dreams, hopes, skills, and knowledge? What do they hope the school will be? We pair that process with qualitative and quantitative data exploration. Brainstorming sessions with families and kids from the feeder schools can also be valuable. Some schools go beyond and have students as full members of the design team and/or the launch team. That involvement varies depending on each school's constraints.

> **ANNA'S ONE GOOD QUESTION:** Does this new design create opportunities for kids or does this design prove or support an adult's idea?

ONE GOOD QUESTION WITH CONNIE K. CHUNG: HOW CAN WE BUILD SYSTEMS TO SUPPORT POWERFUL LEARNING? (USA)

I met Connie K. Chung at the United World College (UWC) Congress in 2016. The UWC Congress happens every few years as a way to bring together different stakeholders from across the global UWC community to reflect on the needs and strategic direction of the movement. Connie and I were both outsiders to the UWC community; most people at the Congress were alumni, board, staff, or students. I went to the Congress to connect with other members of a nascent Cuba National Committee that is dedicated to identifying and supporting Cuban nationals in the application process. My lens was primarily an equity and access one — what are systemic barriers for Black and Latinx students to attend UWC campuses. Connie came to the Congress more focused on pedagogy and how the UWC model provided for truly holistic learning. It wasn't until after our interview that I learned that Connie is one of the United States' foremost experts on the United Nations' Sustainable Development Goals (SDGs), specifically Education 2030. Since our interview, Connie has co-edited the book *Teaching and Learning for the Twenty-first Century: Educational Goals, Policies, and Curricula from Six Nations* (Harvard Education Press, 2016).

In what ways do our investments in education reveal our beliefs about the next generation's role in the world?

Different communities are investing in their young people in different kinds of ways. Who is deciding how the investment is made is also an indicator of what we value in the next generation. Young people's voices and even teachers' voices can be included on a larger scale. Going forward, given the rapid shifts of what we need to teach our young people, and the current emphasis on personalized learning, those two groups of people are essential to include in deciding what future investments might be.

A good investment requires a diversified portfolio. We're going to need a diversified portfolio to figure out what we're doing for the future. Much of our current investments are in developing cognition. So much of how we have invested our money, energy, time, human resources, attention, and discourse has recently been around testing. I do think testing does help for accountability, transparency, and promoting quality to a certain degree. But it's not enough. We need more investments in the following:

- Developing a more holistic, child-centered vision and purpose for education.
- Developing systems that are responsive to the needs of the present and the future.
- Strategizing and visioneering to create systems in which parts work together.
- Obtaining consistent, impactful leadership. Average turnover for superintendents in the US is nearly three years, which isn't enough to develop sustainable, responsive, or adequate systems for what the students need.
- Creating adequate space, time, and resources for teachers to learn while they are teaching. The technology and content is changing so rapidly that it requires continual learning, even for teachers.

We need to develop systems to learn from each other. I know lots of great examples of powerful teachers, schools, and networks like United World College (UWC), EL Education (EL), and High Tech High (HTH) doing wonderful work. But I don't see a lot of investment in ways to systematically identify, catalogue, curate, and make transparent and transferable some of these processes for teachers, school leaders, and heads of systems. What might be sustainable models for teachers to continue to learn in their PLCs, schools, district and region?

What's keeping us from making that kind of investment in the US? It would be helpful to enable cultures and conditions where teachers' voices are heard. I've seen this at EL Education schools in the US. Many of their schools have restructured their school time to enable more teachers to collaborate in interdisciplinary teams and let students do projects in longer blocks of time. Some EL Education schools have even restructured the spaces within the schools for the collaboration to occur. So that work is happening, but it's not happening at a larger scale. In places like EL Education, they have leadership that is listening to teachers and thinking about how to establish the conditions so that the real learning happens. They're not so invested in finding the next silver bullet, but in developing whole school cultures that enable continual learning and growth in community to happen.

In *Teaching and Learning for the Twenty-First Century: Educational Goals, Policies, and Curricula from Six Nations*, one of your findings is that countries emphasize cognitive domains over interpersonal and intrapersonal domains in their K-12 curriculum. Why does that matter?

Learning is cognitive, but it's also social and emotional. For example, we can look at Tony Bryk's work on trust[21] in schools. The places where student achievement increased were places that have a culture of trust. These are environments where people felt able and vulnerable to say, "This is what I need to learn and grow," and felt safe socially and emotionally to do that. And they have communities that supported that vulnerability instead of punishing students into hiding it. Carol Dweck's[22] work is not just about a growth mindset for students but could be applied to teachers as well. The process of learning is not just cerebral; learning is about vulnerability and humility, and it takes place in a supportive and collaborative school culture that listens to, learns from, and challenges its members. The more we acknowledge and understand that, the more we can build our systems to support not just the development of cognition, but also cultures, systems, and relationship building. And that hard work needs to be done now. It's not magic.

I've heard too many times about cases where school districts pivoted and adopted a twenty-first century student-centered curriculum, but did so

---

[21] Bryk, Anthony S., and Barbara Schneider. *Trust in Schools: A Core Resource for Improvement.* New York: Russell Sage Foundation, 2002.

[22] Dweck, Carol. *Mindset: The New Psychology of Success. How We Can Learn to Fulfill Our Potential.* (2006) Random House.

without other support systems and structures to enable that change. But as several educational leaders have noted, "Culture eats policy for breakfast." Even in China, our colleagues also found that, in their innovative school districts, their broader district culture embraces innovations and trying new things. We might continue to recognize and cultivate leaders who pay attention to how to build cultures and environments that enable students and teachers to do this kind of work. We need a shift in the kinds of questions that we're asking, a shift in processes and frameworks, not just in acquiring a new curriculum.

In a nineteenth century factory model of education, where we wanted to get the process right for mass production, education quality was defined by consistency. The twenty-first century education model is a sharing economy in which all people have the ability to be creators. The ability to cultivate systems and cultures that enable that to happen, where people feel empowered and equipped, is perhaps just as important as paying attention to individual components like curriculum. I think the cultural piece can't be emphasized enough — values, attitudes, relationships, and structures. How do we create that kind of environment?

How do we do this without over-testing social-emotional learning? The ultimate assessment is, "Are we going to survive and thrive as a country?"

Have we created students through our school systems who are going to live well together and promote their own and others' well-being? That's the ultimate high-stakes assessment! We may have people who have tested well in schools but may well be failing this real assessment of creating a sustainable future together. This goes back to the purpose of education, which is important to look at as a guide.

We have overemphasized assessment to guide us. Assessment is one indicator for achieving our broader purpose, but we've disproportionately given power to assessment to drive the entire endeavor of education. It's a tool, but testing well is just part, not the entire purpose and end goal of education; personal, social, and global well-being are. OECD is driving towards these broader outcomes with their Education 2030 plan; it focuses more on creating positive value and well-being, for example. UNESCO is also arguing for education to be a critical part of building sustainable futures for everyone on the planet. If that's the case, let's figure out how we can build a better world together using all of our tools and not solely relying on narrow indicators.

CONNIE'S ONE GOOD QUESTION: How do we collect and connect good people who are already doing this work to make it grow exponentially versus linearly?

ONE GOOD QUESTION WITH TONY MONFILETTO: ARE THE RIGHT PEOPLE IN THE EDUCATION REDESIGN PROCESS? (USA)

I can't remember how I first met Tony Monfiletto because we cross paths in several communities and contexts. In one space we may be talking about school design — Tony developed a secondary school with community employment partners in New Mexico. In another space we may be talking about equity in personalized learning contexts. Or I may hear from our shared community in Memphis that he's been asking hard questions about the future of community voice in education. Wherever we are, I always have something new to learn from Tony and his perspective. This interview was no different. Tony has held a wide range of positions in education, from substitute teacher to administrator and now as Executive Director of Future Focused Education. The questions that he asks about school design are deeply rooted in honoring local communities.

In what ways do our investments in education reveal our beliefs about the next generation's role in the world?

Our investment in accountability structure and high-stakes standardized testing reveals the fact that adults think of kids as problems to be solved, rather than assets to be nurtured. In Jal Mehta's, *The Allure of Order*, he outlines how the investment in accountability at the back end of the system is an effort to make up for the fact that we haven't invested as aggressively in the front end. We don't put enough time, energy, or strategy into good school design, preparation of teachers, or capital development. Because we don't put enough resources into those areas, we try to make up for it in accountability structures.

From substitute teacher to education policy, you've worked in practically every level of education impact and have a deep understanding of how all of these roles influence opportunities for all students. What is standing in the way of deeper, effective collaboration for public education in this country?

We were working off of an old industrial model of education and when that industrial model stopped getting results, we had different expectations for what schools could do, but we never changed the design of the schools to catch up to the new expectations. When we didn't change the design of the schools or invest in the people who could populate the new generation of schools, we started accountability structures instead. If we're going to deal with the lack of effective design, it's going to mean dealing with both the accountability structures to make sure that it's rethought around clear design principles. We have to do both at the same time. You can't have accountability structures built around industrial factory schools when that model isn't solving the problem. You have to get both accountability and design right, but now we're not doing either. People are trying to deal with the metrics questions but aren't willing to give up on the design. Even those who are thinking about innovative school design are still doing it within the confines of the existing model, i.e., replacing teachers with blended learning. These are add-ons, not really answering questions for what's happening in the instruction.

Do you think we have the right people in the conversation about school design? I don't. What's happened is that we've let two camps develop: traditional education interest groups/educators versus high-stakes standards educators. The traditional camp is dominated by teacher unions, school administrators, Diane Ravitch, etc., and the high-stakes camp is dominated by those who believe in econometrics. They think that if you get the econometrics right, then align the systems and create the right incentives, everything will come out in the end. The discourse on school design is dominated by those two camps and they're not the right people to be in the conversation. The trappings of the existing system make it difficult for both camps to imagine anything else. We need youth development advocates, neuroscientists, community leaders who are not from the education sector, social service providers who understand cognitive and non-cognitive human development — those are the people who ought to be in the conversations. If we had them in the discussion and designed backwards, we'd have a much differently designed school than our current models. At Leadership High School Network in Albuquerque, we operate and founded a network of schools built around three pillars: learning by doing, community engagement, and 360-degree support for kids and families. All pillars are equally important, and they all hold up the institution. What we found is, when any two of the three pillars converge, the impact for kids is exponential. It's the convergence that creates the impact, but they have to be seen as equal partners in their work in the schools.

> **TONY'S ONE GOOD QUESTION:** Can we give the community a new mental model for what school can look like? And then, can we create a new assessment system that allows for people to have confidence in that new model?

ONE GOOD QUESTION WITH SAKU TUOMINEN: NEXT 100 YEARS OF FINNISH EDUCATION (FINLAND)

I first met Saku Tuominen in a café in Helsinki. I knew very little about Saku's professional trajectory and he probably knew less about mine. This was another opportunity to enter the conversation with wonder. Saku is most known as a television producer in Finland who happens to be a restaurateur, author, and expert on developing effective office culture. Mutual friends knew about my work in global education and recommended that we connect. His latest project, HundrED, was centered on scaling innovation in K-12 schools and he had an ambitious plan to start with Finnish educators and eventually engage educators from all over the globe.

In what ways do our investments in education reveal our beliefs about the next generation's role in the world?

What education expenditures tell us about Finland: we invest significantly in education because everyone in Finland feels it's important; however, the discussion we refuse to have is the why? What is the essence of education, the purpose of schools?

In Finland, we love solid hard work, but we tend to be risk-averse in our work, reacting to crises well, but not developing longer vision when systems function well. I feel that even our Prime Minister should take the opportunity of our new curriculum to be visionary, and ask four essential questions to inform how we redesign education in our country:

1. What are the skills kids should learn at school?
2. How should they learn those skills?
3. Who should be the people facilitating the learning process? Is it teachers and teachers only? What is the role of young people? Old people? Companies? Parents?

126

4. Where should the learning take place? Should it be only in schools? In the city? In the parks? In society? Via internet platforms?

Based on the answers to these questions, we should ask what governments, companies, and cities are responsible for doing to recreate our education ecosystem.

In your Scool project, you've identified the biggest need as helping schools change and providing platforms for change at the student, teacher, school, and system level. Why do you think it can be difficult for schools to adopt change? What are the early learnings about where change is most impactful, at the student, teacher, classroom, school, or system level?

In order for human beings to change, they must first believe that change is possible. In this case, we must believe that we can change the way we educate and how our schools are structured. Then we have to have the courage, the mental toughness, and resources to do the work of change.

We ask ourselves how we can be certain that the new things we try in schools will work. Well, the honest answer is that we don't yet know, but how can we be certain that the things we do in schools today are relevant from the perspective of 2030? We don't know that either. The best way to encourage change is to redefine failure. We are trying new things and none of the outcomes are failure if we're learning from the results. In 2016, Finland launched a new curriculum that included freedom for teachers and schools to define teaching, but there was no discussion about the evaluation system. This ambiguity fostered a disincentive to actually try anything new. If schools or teachers take the freedom to teach curiosity and creativity, but then students are only measured on math and physics, there's an inherent tension.

With the Scool project, our mission is to help schools change. Culturally, not enough Finns are risk-takers and entrepreneurs. Although the new curriculum encouraged more teacher freedom, not all teachers were likely to exercise it. We needed to do a massive empowerment campaign for teachers, showing them that it's great to take risks, to make mistakes. The HundrED project of Scool was designed to support teachers' risk-taking by giving them the best platforms to share new ideas and best practices in classrooms just like theirs.

During our site visits across Finland, we've been to schools that are doing amazing things with average budgets. In one school, a teacher refuses to give any grades to any students; students themselves are giving the grades. The biggest problem is that the best kids hesitate to give themselves the best grades that they deserve. In another school, the teachers no longer purchase educational materials, and instead, they are creating their own with students. Teachers help guide the content and the context for bookmaking about the topic of study. In some instances, they may even sell the books to others as resources. In a third school, students took responsibility for a bullying problem. The school decided to take teachers completely out of the equation and gave the responsibility of solving this problem to the oldest students in the primary school. As a result of the student-led interventions, all of the difficulties disappeared. This is the area that is getting me most excited because if you can tell these stories of success within the same regular conditions, it gives more credit for other schools to try something new. These three examples illustrate the essence of the future of schools: putting students at the center of problem-solving for their own learning.

What's the key commonality in these schools? It's like what happens in any great company—you have to have a great principal in place. One teacher can make changes in one class, but over time it becomes more complicated. It's all about principal leadership because they inspire teachers to try innovations, and then they celebrate and share the gains that teachers have made with the greater community.

SAKU'S ONE GOOD QUESTION: What is the point of school?

ONE GOOD QUESTION WITH NOELLE LIM: WHAT STEAM COULD MEAN FOR MALAYSIA (MALAYSIA)

When I met Noelle Lim, she was working in Singapore and observing the stark education differences between that country and Malaysia, her home. Singaporean students score consistently higher than the OECD average on all PISA[23] assessments. Whereas in Malaysia, not only do students consistently score below the OECD (Organisation for Economic Co-operation and Development) average, but there is also a significant performance gap where students from higher socioeconomic backgrounds greatly outperform their peers from lower socioeconomic backgrounds.

At the time of our interview, Noelle had worked in the finance industry in Malaysia and Singapore, hosted business radio shows, and written for Forbes Asia. Based on her professional background, I was surprised to hear her advocate for more arts in school.

In what ways do our investments in education reveal our beliefs about the next generation's role in the world?

In Malaysia, education takes the lion's share in the government budget, so it's clear the government is fairly serious about it. One reason is cultural — our society prizes good education — and another is that Malaysia relies on foreign investments, so it's an open economy that needs to have a globally competent workforce.

Parents are serious about education too. For example, in Malaysia and developed countries of Asia, it's a norm for parents who have the means to pay for their child to attend supplementary classes conducted by private tutors.

---

[23] Programme for International Student Assessment is administered every three years. Due to COVID-19, the next PISA exams will be held in 2022 and 2025.

However, I think parents pay for these classes, not in hope their child will become the next Nobel Prize winner, but to pass the national exams with straight As. It's assumed that if you do this, you can perhaps win a scholarship or get a place in a good university, and you'll be set for life.

It appears however, that our education system isn't really working out for boys. Girls outperform boys in maths and science unlike international norms. And in public universities, girls account for 70% of the intake. Our education blueprint has highlighted the risk of "lost boys." Given the patriarchal expectations within conservative communities, I wonder what impact this achievement gap will have on the next generation.

During your Eisenhower Fellowship, you came to the United States to learn more about education entrepreneurship. How will your school design reflect learning and innovation from both countries?

The PISA[24] rankings show that Malaysia's education system is in the bottom third (yet neighbor Singapore is number one), and TIMSS[25] show that Malaysia is below average international standards (it was above average in the 1990s). It appears to be an uphill task for Malaysia to catch up. I don't think we need to aspire to be number one but aim to be in the top quartile. And I think we're capable of doing that because our society values education. Malaysian schools need to upgrade the content of what they are teaching. For instance, an online, centralized database of teaching notes with suggested pedagogy and updates could help the schools.

Secondly, the current method of teaching in Malaysia, and indeed still in many countries, is done in silo. We don't help students connect dots, and there's a push for STEM in Malaysia. I believe the focus has to shift to STEAM instead with subjects to be taught in an interdisciplinary way. Finding solutions to complex problems in the world requires a more comprehensive way of thinking, and a combination of science and arts/humanities. Innovations too; for example, the iPad is a marriage of tech prowess and design.

---

[24] Programme for International Student Assessment. OECD. https://www.oecd.org/pisa/ Accessed March 2016.

[25] Mullis, I. V. S., Martin, M. O., Foy, P., Kelly, D. L., & Fishbein, B. (2020). TIMSS 2019 International Results in Mathematics and Science. Retrieved from Boston College, TIMSS & PIRLS International Study Center website: https://timssandpirls.bc.edu/timss2019/international-results/

In the United States, I visited two schools that are shifting from STEM to STEAM and incorporating more holistic offerings such as entrepreneurship and liberal arts: North Carolina School of Science and Mathematics and Illinois Mathematics and Science Academy. I chose those schools because the Ministry of Education from Singapore and China frequently visit them. These public schools have strong academic performance, particularly in STEM, and selective admissions. At the North Carolina campus, Chancellor Todd Roberts has a degree in English and believes in a well-rounded education. Illinois Math and Science is developing an entrepreneurship thread. They are mobilizing their alumni base and drawing them in to mentor students and provide internships in start-ups in Chicago. These are gradual processes, to move towards STEAM instructional expectations.

Two questions that I asked almost all schools I visited were, "What is the purpose of a school? What is the purpose of education?" Apart from ensuring children are literate and know their sums, I believe it's about helping the student discover a range of possible interests, and to help the child choose which path to pursue and to arm him with the relevant information. This means schools have to give the child opportunities to work on projects of personal interests like capstone projects. Once the child finds his interest, there is no looking back. Many successful people I've interviewed say that what they do is their passion and luck of course helps. Either they found their passion by accident or were drawn to it by a mentor. I think schools can play a bigger role in helping children find their passions.

I also believe schools should produce people who will develop the agency, aptitude, and desire to want to solve complex problems. It's not just to pass exams, but to create the next generation of scientists, artists, makers, entrepreneurs, and leaders.

NOELLE'S ONE GOOD QUESTION: How well does our education system in Malaysia engage boys?

ONE GOOD QUESTION WITH AYLON SAMOUHA: IS THERE A SILVER BULLET FOR THE FUTURE OF "SCHOOL"? (USA)

When I interviewed Aylon Samouha, he and Jeff Wetzler had recently founded Transcend, a nonprofit education consulting group. They had a vision for school redesign that engaged young people, parents, teachers, administrators, and community partners. I spent a few months in 2016 consulting with them on their early portfolio development and started to learn what redesign meant from their perspective. A year or so later, I was able to observe one of their community design sessions in Memphis, and it was the first time that I saw design thinking[26] in action. What I appreciated most was how the process democratized ideation and problem-solving. Design thinking went beyond getting proximate with young people to really centering their voice in the design of their learning experience. In this interview, Aylon gives us a window into his wonderings, early experiences with design thinking, and how they led him to develop Transcend.

In what ways do our investments in education reveal our beliefs about the next generation's role in the world?

Thankfully, there is a lot of investment in education, both public and philanthropic dollars. The sheer quantity of investment is a clear signal — we believe that our generation plays a critical role in the future world and deserves deep investment. That said, where does it go? There are lots of human capital investments that

---

[26] Design thinking is a human-centered process for creative problem-solving that dates back to the 1970s.

funders are making in all sorts of ways to attract, evaluate, and train educators. These investments are animated by a critical need in creating great learning environments; namely, kids need caring adults around them who are effective at teaching, coaching, motivating, etc.

On the other hand, human capital funding by itself may unintentionally reinforce the idea that the only, or best, way for kids to learn is through teacher-centric models where students have little agency over their own learning. With School in the Cloud, Sugata Mitra challenges the role of educators in the learning process. Basically, he was a web developer who said, "What would happen if I just put a computer in the wall here?" in a low-income neighborhood in India. Kids started using it and they had never touched a computer before. They looked up stuff and started learning things. Then he said, let me do it someplace where there aren't a bunch of techies around. And this time he gave the users a question to figure out. When he asked for their feedback, they said "We have to learn English in order to use it." And they actually did learn English to figure out how to keep accessing the tool! This is an extreme but very instructive example that, with the right tools and motivations, students will self-direct their own learning. So we have to ask ourselves, is it enough to invest in human capital when the underlying traditional model, by its design, under-leverages the innate motivation of students to self-direct their learning? And what might that say about how we conceive of their place in the world?

Another important and laudable category of investments go towards scaling "good schools." This comes from a very good place and should continue — if we're seeing a good learning environment in one place, we should try to replicate that in more communities, especially where educational opportunities are poor. That said, an unintended consequence of scale investments is that half-baked things grow before they're really proven, and successful operators sometimes grow faster than the quality can keep up.

Scaling education models is an efficiency play and lots of students and families have had significantly better education choices and experiences as a result of these investments. Counting and expanding "quality seats" is critical work. That said, what unintended narratives might animate these investments? To what extent are we saying that we need quality seats so that our students can be "competitive" in the global marketplace? Instead, how might we expand quality seats while reinforcing a narrative that an American student from New Orleans should be working with her brothers and sisters in China to make the world a better place and not merely trying to "outcompete" them? And when we scale into new communities quickly, to what extent are we "going fast alone versus going further together?" This is all a tricky balancing act and I'm heartened to see so many "in this work" asking these questions more often and more publicly.

Education leaders around the world are asking themselves, "What's next?" Our industrial model of education is no longer preparing youth for today's careers or knowledge economy. Is there a single answer, a silver bullet that will emerge in the next iteration of "school?"

I definitely don't think there is a silver bullet in terms of one type of school or kind of pedagogy. But there are some very provocative ideas and shifts that I think will help us massively improve learning across the world. Right now, I'm enthralled by Todd Rose's work and *The End of Average*. A core premise of this book is that "any system that is trying to fit the individual is actually doomed to fail." Waking up from what he calls the "myth of average" seems critical to redesigning the traditional model which essentially holds the "average" student as a foundational principle. And just like there is no average student, there are no average communities. Taken together, we need to build models that respect and leverage the uniqueness of each student, and we need to scale those models and ideas in ways that communities can adopt and adapt into to fit their unique values, assets, etc. Generic, cookie-cutter replication may work for enterprises where people have very basic expectations and where the stakes are low (i.e., Starbucks, Target). We don't want schools or learning experiences to be like that. Communities creating and adapting school models for their context — school models that provide students to adapt and create learning for themselves... maybe that's a silver bullet?

Relatedly, I'm getting more and more excited about the potential of truly leveraging learning science to advance the way that we construct learning experiences. Research on learning and motivation point to new insights every year — and we need to systematically use these insights in real daily learning environments! To do this right now, educators, who are already stretched in terms of capacity, would need to wade through endless research papers, discern the "usable knowledge" and then figure out how to apply that knowledge with students. What would it mean for us to systematically create the bridge between research and application? What if people designing learning experiences could benefit from, and contribute to, an ever-growing learning agenda for the field? What if more "learning engineers" were building and iterating school model components based on the science that educators could readily adapt into their communities? Ok, maybe that's another silver bullet after all!

AYLON'S ONE GOOD QUESTION: How can we ensure that schools are wildly motivating for all students?

ONE GOOD QUESTION WITH TOM VANDER ARK: CAN DESIGN THINKING & RETHINKING SCALE BOOST EDUCATION EQUITY? (USA)

When I learned that Tom Vander Ark was the keynote speaker for the 2015 Missouri Charter Public School Association annual conference, I reached out to his team to invite him to a one good question interview. I was most familiar with his 2014 book *Smart Cities That Work for Everyone: 7 Keys to Education and Employment*. I was increasingly interested in how the future of education would intersect with other sectors and thought he would have a unique take on my wondering. We met in the bar of the hotel lobby before his keynote address and shared stories.

One of the things that I enjoyed most in this interview series was opportunities like this one when I didn't know enough about the leader's career to be intimidated or overly cautious when interviewing them. When I started our interview, Tom was the Getting Smart guy. I learned in our conversation that he was at the forefront of 1:1 computer models[27], the first Executive Director of Education at the Bill & Melinda Gates Foundation, and a national expert on federal programs for school accountability. Knowing less about a person's path can release the pressure of how you assume they might answer your question. That was certainly the case for this interview with Tom Vander Ark.

In what ways do our investments in education reveal our beliefs about the next generation's role in the world?

We've inherited a sedimentary system made up of a series of 100 years of

---

[27] One device (usually a laptop computer) for every student. This was a departure from the previous generation of fixed computer labs or mobile laptop carts.

laws and policies and practices that for us in the US are federal, state, and local. This is in contrast to an engineered system designed to produce a set of outcomes. So, that's the first problem: our investments, speaking about our public education system writ large, are a product of a democratic process and not a design system. It's many and mixed intentions, it is compromises both good and bad, it is consequences both intended and unintended, working itself out over time.

The US has a number of anachronistic fixations with local control and reliable and valid assessments. This fixation has the advantage of vesting investments closest to the kids, but the disadvantage of it is linking it to community wealth. This is a great example of a well-intentioned design principle that has produced outrageous inequities in US education. Education funding and, to some extent, quality are now ZIP code specific because we vested power in local governments.

When Arne Duncan announced his departure as Secretary of Education, I wrote a blog post suggesting that we mark that day as the end of standards-based reform. From Dick Reilly to Arne Duncan, we had an unusual twenty-year arc in the US, where the federal government had an unusually strong influence from a policy (No Child Left Behind (NCLB)) and investment standpoint (i.e., American Recovery and Reinvestment Act of 2009 (ARRA), Race to the Top). It was a great moment in US education that marked a national, bipartisan consensus for equity. As a country, we could no longer sit by and accept chronic failure for our nation's children.

NCLB was designed as a framework for school accountability to make sure that every family had access to good educational options. In retrospect, almost everyone agrees that the steps and measures used were flawed, but if we had used an iterative development process — kept what was good and fixed the obvious problem — the country would be in a better place. One of the problems with NCLB was that, when faced with a choice between measuring proficiency or measuring growth, we latched on to proficiency because it was easy to measure with valid assessments. We largely ignored growth in the law and now we can see the consequences of it. NCLB had a strong focus on getting underperforming kids to grade level which created two unintended consequences: it discouraged schools from teaching students who were furthest behind (over age, undercredited), and weaker administrators fixated on the test. Rather than offering a rich, full, inspiring education, they offered test prep. Not only did that not produce lasting academic results for kids, but it also led to educators trying to game the test, with examples of cheating and embezzlement in the worst cases.

In the past few years we've seen funders, media, and eventually schools rally around the next big tech innovation (1:1, MOOC (Massive Open Online Courses), coding, etc). How much does the next big tool matter for lasting academic outcomes for all students?

The reason that I'm so passionate about public education and investment in innovation is because I think that it's the fastest path to quality and access to quality in the US and internationally. In my previous Ed Reformer blog, I wrote about education reform, making the system that we have better. Getting Smart reflects the new imperative, for every family and neighborhood around the world, to get smart fast. I'm concerned that things will get better faster for young people who have engaged and supportive adults in their lives. I'm worried about young people who don't have engaged parents/adults in their lives. Parents who get powerful learning are raising confident, equipped, well-informed young people.

Innovation is critically important to improving access and quality. It's why I'm really optimistic that things will get better, faster in the US and accelerate international change as well. In the US, innovation investment allows us a design opportunity. The design experience that I'm most passionate about is people who are conceptualizing LX+IT (learner experience + integrated information technology). They're not just developing new school models but also integrating information systems and student access devices. We're still in the early innings now of new tools and new schools. There are thousands of good new schools, but there are only dozens of schools that are doing this fundamental design work of reconceptualizing learning environments and learning sequences and the tools that go with it. This is the opportunity of our time: to find ways to scale both the work and the number of folks benefitting from it worldwide.

Internationally, we have the first chance in history to offer every young person on the planet a great education. When we first started investing in scalable models in the US, funders and founders had grand ambitions that assumed linear replication. Over time, we've learned that scaling nationally or internationally is much harder than maintaining strong regional programs and outcomes. We're starting to see a shift in replication and inspiration across geographies. Take

Rocketship Schools for example. They run an amazing model that everyone has flocked to see in the past few years. Among the visitors were two young MBAs from Johannesburg, who took the lessons learned from Rocketship and created SPARK Schools in Johannesburg. SPARK is as good a blended learning model as I've seen anywhere on the planet. Rocketship didn't have to cross the ocean for that to happen and now students in South Africa are benefitting from a model that was created in the US.

Summit Public Schools has taken a different approach to scaling ideas before scaling schools. In 2015, they had about nineteen school partners with their Basecamp model. They created a powerful Personalized Learning Platform, partnered with Facebook and Stanford to figure out how to scale it for broader use, and now team with schools across the country to implement this pedagogy into existing models. We hope that hundreds of schools benefit from their fundamental design work. Seeing these types of growth gives me a tremendous sense of optimism that things can get better worldwide faster than most people realize.

TOM'S ONE GOOD QUESTION: Will we actually achieve equitable education access?

WHAT ARE YOU WONDERING?

TOM WONDERS: Will we actually achieve equitable education access?

CONNIE WONDERS: How do we collect and connect good people who are already doing this work to make it grow exponentially rather than linearly?

TONY WONDERS: Can we give the community a new mental model for what school can look like? And then, can we create a new assessment system that allows for people to have confidence in that new model?

AYLON WONDERS: How can we ensure that schools are wildly motivating for all students?

SAKU WONDERS: What is the point of school?

NOELLE WONDERS: How well does our education system in Malaysia engage boys?

ANNA WONDERS: Does this new school design create opportunities for kids or does this design prove or support an adult's idea?

When you think about designing new types of school or instructional models, which elements of the status quo do you want to challenge? What did you already know about school design that was challenged here?

As you reflect on your one good question —

- Think about your audience: Which voices were missing from this chapter? Who are the experts for your wondering?
- Think about your context: What new type of school or instructional model would matter most for your local needs?
- Think about your timing: Are you trying to get clarity on what has occurred or on what could be?

WHY LANGUAGE MATTERS

CHAPTER 5

Bilingual/Bilingüe

BY RHINA P. ESPAILLAT

My father liked them separate, one there,
one here (allá y aquí), as if aware

that words might cut in two his daughter's heart
(el corazón) and lock the alien part

to what he was — his memory, his name
(su nombre) — with a key he could not claim.

"English outside this door, Spanish inside,"
he said, "y basta." But who can divide

the world, the word (mundo y palabra) from
any child? I knew how to be dumb

and stubborn (testaruda); late, in bed,
I hoarded secret syllables I read

until my tongue (mi lengua) learned to run
where his stumbled. And still the heart was one.

I like to think he knew that, even when,
proud (orgulloso) of his daughter's pen,

he stood outside mis versos, half in fear
of words he loved but wanted not to hear.

Rhina P. Espaillat, "Bilingual/Bilingüe" from Where Horizons Go
(Kirksville, MO: New Odyssey Books, 1998).
Reprinted with the permission of the author.

The United States does not have an official language. What this country does have, is a systemic history of extinguishing every language other than English. State legislatures, schools, education agencies, and education budgets have played a key role in centering English as the language of power in the United States. At the turn of the twentieth century, the US government invested in Native American boarding schools, also known as Indian Residential Schools, designed to assimilate Indigenous people to white culture and extinguish their use of Native languages. Through World War I, individual territories, states, cities, parishes, and counties invoked their rights to either protect or prohibit regionally important languages like French in Louisiana, German throughout the Northeast and Midwest, Spanish in California and Puerto Rico, Hawai'ian in Hawai'i, and Tagalog in the Philippines.

In this chapter, leaders speak less about the official language policies and economic investment in English and more about the tensions in contemporary language pedagogies and multilingual education. Like in Espaillat's poem, accessing school as a multilingual person in the US is already fraught with generational pressure and contradictions. Karen Beeman (USA) explores what a monolingual education system gets right and wrong about the ways that multilingual people speak and learn. Deanne Thomas (New Zealand) questions how the investments in bilingual, bicultural New Zealand contribute to Māori leadership opportunities. Suzanne Talhouk (Lebanon) explores how multilingual people demote their ethnic language in public spaces. Dr. Fred Genesee (Canada) defends the right of "struggling students" to access language immersion programs, and Dr. Elvira Souza Lima (Brazil) teases out the distinctions between oracy and literacy and how formal instruction impacts both.

ONE GOOD QUESTION WITH KAREN BEEMAN: HOW BILITERACY SUPPORTS SOCIAL JUSTICE FOR ALL (USA)

I first heard Karen Beeman speak at the Brazilian Immersion Conference in 2015. Karen gave a workshop that challenged my binary thinking about multilingualism and proficiency. I had just spent eight years leading a network of language immersion schools and emphasizing the importance of total language immersion practices. In my weekly talks with prospective parents, I consistently gave examples of how new students would mix their home language and instructional language in the same sentence. I wanted parents to be prepared for that when their children came home speaking spanglish, franglais, or chinglish. In that same conversation, I would also narrate for families when they could expect to hear their children separate the two languages and their contexts. My goal was to reassure monolingual English-speaking families about the immersion process. It worked! Every year newly enrolled families would let me know when their children were mixing languages and when they started to separate them out. These were two early signs of language proficiency.

What Karen challenged me on was less about how monolingual English-speakers experienced proficiency in a language immersion context, but how young people growing up in bilingual households had the right to a different language trajectory. I see my own children and their language use in Karen's work. She and I followed up with this interview a few weeks after that conference and as a bilingual parent, I am still learning from her example.

"Voy a una party con mi broder." When Karen Beeman gave this example of a typical statement from a bilingual student, the room of language immersion educators nodded and smiled in agreement. We had all heard our students mix languages before. But Beeman's point was not about the typical interlanguage that occurs during language acquisition. Her example was of children whose first language is bilingual. Kids who inherit this natural mix from their bilingual homes and communities and learn later, usually in school, to separate the two languages.

In her practice at the Center for Teaching for Biliteracy, Beeman contends that we need to acknowledge that while bilingualism is a starting point for many of our students, it is not the anticipated outcome. She prides herself in making education research accessible for K-12 teachers and this workshop exemplified that belief. Just a few minutes into her talk, Karen had the audience building linguistic bridges between Portuguese and English to understand how the practice would support student-constructed learning. To the untrained eye, bridges look like translations, and Beeman knew that once teachers created their own bridges, they would see the value in leading their students through this construction.

Karen has dedicated her career to elevating and protecting the status of minority language in a majority language education system, specifically Spanish in the US. When I sat down with her to talk about her one good question, I assumed that her focus would be on investing in language education. What I learned, however, was far more about her vision for all youth in our country. Karen grew up the child of white Americans in Mexico and when she moved to the States for university, she had the unique perspective of appearing American and having strong linguistic and cultural identity in Mexico and Mexican Spanish. Karen quickly became an education advocate for bilingualism and champion for elevating the status of Spanish in urban communities with significant Hispanic populations.

Karen's inquiry starts from that place of language specific, culture-specific instructional practice and quickly progresses to questions of social justice and equity: How are we preparing minoritized students to see themselves in the culture of power? For the 71% of ELL youth who speak Spanish[28], access to bilingual academic communities that support literacy in both languages means that they get to comfortably exist in majority culture.

> "When students feel visible and what is going on in school matches who they are, we reach their potential."
>
> – Karen Beeman

---

[28] Ruiz Soto, Ariel G., Sarah Hooker; and Jeanne Bataloca. 2015 *Top Languages Spoken by English Language Learners Nationally and by State.* Washington, DC: Migration Policy Institute

For bilingual and heritage students, this visibility begins with equal access to and respect for their home languages. Karen is agnostic about the type of academic model schools choose. Traditional bilingual, dual language, and two-way immersion programs are all built around English language expectations. What makes the biggest difference? Looking beyond the monolingual perspective and the English dominant perspective. "We cannot use English as our paradigm for what we do in the other language," Karen insists.

With respect to the pedagogy and materials in current Spanish-language programs, Beeman contends that we're creating our own problem. Most texts in bilingual classrooms (fiction, non-fiction, and academic) are translations into the non-English language. This means that they are translating English grammar and syntax progressions into a language with completely different rules. Bilingual students may miss out on natural, age-appropriate expressions in Spanish and often misunderstand the cultural context of a translated story. Beeman traveled to Mexico for years and brought back authentic children's literature in Spanish, but those texts also didn't work for her bilingual American students. In written texts, the academic grammar, vocabulary, and syntax is at a higher register than oral language. Bilingual students whose Spanish-dominant parents may not be literate in Spanish, then have little understanding of the "authentic" text.

What Beeman experienced was that neither monolingual context worked for bilingual students. If we are to capture bilingual students' full potential, we need a third way. Enter language bridges: a constructivist approach that showcases the background knowledge and expertise of the students and allows them to access the curriculum and complex ideas in the majority language. Beeman then takes this perspective outside of the classroom; we need to stop imposing monolingual perspectives on education policy, pedagogy, and educator training.

When we recognize that — 1. We have a language of power (academic register of English) and a culture of power (middle-class, European-influenced discourse) that influence all of our instruction, and 2. Our country is becoming increasingly diverse linguistically, ethnically, and socially — we quickly understand that the need for all types of language and culture bridges in our instructional practice encompasses the majority of the country.

Whether we're addressing socioeconomic status, home language, or student identity, most of our students walk into their classrooms as the "other" in the curriculum. Looking at the trends for an increasingly diverse population in the US, we have to ask ourselves what happens when our education system doesn't embed respect for minoritized cultures.

> **KAREN'S ONE GOOD QUESTION:** "How can a student's experience build on his/her fount of knowledge, both linguistic and cultural?"

ONE GOOD QUESTION WITH SUZANNE TALHOUK: IS ACADEMIC LANGUAGE ENOUGH? A LOOK AT SOCIAL CAPITAL AND MINORITIZED LANGUAGES (LEBANON)

When I first listened to Suzanne Talhouk's TEDxBeirut Talk "Don't Kill Your Language," I selected the Brazilian Portugese subtitles. I had been learning Portuguese for the past three months and it made sense to practice my reading comprehension. But I mostly chose Portuguese because out of the twenty-eight subtitles possible, my heritage language, French, wasn't an option. What an ironic way to begin a reflection on the importance of language protectionism!

As a language advocate, I'm accustomed to language protectionism arguments, but what I appreciate most about Talhouk's work is that she isn't preaching to the choir at an academic conference. She originally gave this talk at TEDxBeirut and was admonishing her peers for elevating the status of English and French over Arabic. Talhouk gives familiar positions about native language fluency supporting mastery of additional languages[29] and the emotional link to language and memory[30]. These are widespread logical reasons that we should maintain our heritage languages. Talhouk herself is a poet and also invokes Khalil Gibran's work and complexity of thought in their language. Essentially her argument is that Lebanese people are deciding that their language is less professionally and artistically valuable

---

[29] Cummins, Jim. *Language, Power, and Pedagogy: Bilingual Children in the Crossfire.* Clevedon [England]: Multilingual Matters, 2000.

[30] Schroeder, Scott and Marian, Viorica. "A bilingual advantage for episodic memory in older adults." *Journal of Cognitive Psychology*, vol. 24, no. 5, 2012. pp 591-601.

than English and French. She urges her peers to publish research, create art, and engage deeply in their language.

In the late 1960s and early 1970s, four minoritized language communities were starting language revitalization efforts to keep their local languages from going extinct. Cajun activists in my native Louisiana founded CODOFIL: *Conseil pour le développement du Français en Louisiane* to provide early education access in French and policy advocacy for Cajun and Creole Kouri-Vini speakers. In Hawai'i, Larry Kimura started interviewing elders in the first native Hawai'ian language radio program, *Ka Leo Hawai'i*, and anchored language learning in the Hawai'ian cultural renaissance. In 1971, New Zealand recognized that *te reo maori* was also on the brink of extinction. By the late 1970s, the country had established their first Kōhanga Reo — preschool programs taught entirely in *te reo maori*.

Picture the language revitalization platform as a three-legged table: policy, education access, and social capital. Louisiana, Hawai'i, and New Zealand all have similarly strong policy and education access for their heritage languages. Louisiana has twenty-six French immersion schools across eight parishes. Hawai'i currently has the largest number of high school language immersion programs in the United States. In New Zealand it is possible to study from nursery school through university and receive all of your instruction in *te reo maori*. Of these three communities, New Zealand has made the greatest advances in their third prong: social capital of the minoritized language.

In my parents' generation, we have artists and language activists like Zachary Richard and David Chéramie, who committed to writing in French before, and in great anticipation that we would eventually be able to understand their work *in our language*. They were sowing the seeds for social capital and heritage language legacy. Where New Zealand has created more momentum is in inspiring my generation of artists to be equally committed to language activism. Māori Television (especially their Te Reo channel) and Huia Publishing are institutional examples of promoting social capital of the minoritized language. They produce a wide range of programs and texts, and develop Maori-speaking artists to reach broader audiences in *te reo*. Rob Ruha is a contemporary singer-songwriter, who writes traditional waitas, choreographs *kapa haka* and writes pop songs in *te reo maori*. He believes strongly that he is writing in *te reo* to reflect our generation's experiences and inspire our children's generation to enjoy and value *te reo*.

My children are used to the fact that, whenever given the choice of language, we choose French. From the check-out at Home Depot and the ATM to our movie audio tracks, musicians, and greeting cards, we're intentional about making memories in our language. Speaking and, certainly, raising my children in a minoritized language in the US requires an effort on my part. The irony is not lost on me though, that I'm writing this book in English and not French. Duly noted.

If you are a champion for your minoritized language, ask yourself, "Who are the artists, poets, singers and actors who are carrying the social status of your language for the next generations?" Then ask what legacy you are leaving the next generation now via social media platforms that will keep your language relevant? Talhouk cautions Arabic-speakers in their use of social media. She gives the example of transliterating an Arabic word in a tweet.

> "Whatever you do, don't write Arabic in Roman characters! That's a disaster! It's not a language."
>
> - Suzanne Talhouk

Chinese, Japanese, Korean and Hindi are just a handful of languages that succumbed to Roman script long before the influence of social media. On that point, she may be fighting a lost battle. I would love to follow Suzanne on Twitter, but, as you can imagine, her feed is entirely in Arabic.

ONE GOOD QUESTION WITH DR. FRED GENESEE: DO STRUGGLING LEARNERS BELONG IN LANGUAGE IMMERSION PROGRAMS? (CANADA)

Yes. *But what about the students who have weak L1[31] skills?* Them too. *Our students in poverty don't have the home support to be successful in language immersion. Isn't this a hardship for them?* Nope. *These students need longer time to get academic concepts, won't language immersion delay them in comparison to their peers?* Uh, still no.

Dr. Fred Genesee has been researching bilingual and multilingual development in youth for nearly fifty years. He is one of the most respected and cited voices in the global language immersion community. Genesee's opening keynote for the Brazilian Immersion Conference was about the "struggling" learner in immersion settings. In North America, language immersion education urges us to be more inclusive of children from minoritized ethnic communities, children in lower socioeconomic environments, and students with differentiated learning needs. I appreciate Genesee's keynote even more in the Brazilian context, where virtually all of their language immersion programs are in independent schools that serve affluent, majority culture kids. All educators need reminders and inspiration that increase their expectations for all students.

Genesee's research addresses the dissonance between popular thought and research implications for language immersion. Common sense argues that language immersion is not successful for students with perceived hardship: academic delays, low socioeconomic status, new or poor speakers of the majority language. Why add to their struggle? Genesee compares language immersion

---

[31] L1 refers to your first or native language, the one that you've been exposed to since birth.

students with similar demographics of non-immersion students and native speakers of the immersion language. His results consistently demonstrate that L1 performance, when compared with peers in the control group, are not diminished for "struggling" students (Genesee, 1992; 2007; Genesee, Paradis, & Crago, 2004).

> "It's important to believe that what we're doing is right. If deep down teachers worry about [whether these kids should be in language immersion], it compromises their students' performance."
>
> — Dr. Fred Genesee

The primary message of Genesee's talk was that building strong literacy skills in L2[32] not only supports literacy development in L1, but more importantly, it increases student access to and success in the academic curriculum. Students in language immersion are expected to study complex academic topics in the immersion language by the end of elementary schools. The primary academic reason that students leave language immersion programs in public schools in Canada, is due to reading difficulty and related frustration in the academic curriculum. Committing to and developing literacy skills in L2 unlocks deeper learning for students over time.

Genesee addressed the four most common questions raised by language immersion educators:

1. What levels of proficiency in L1 and L2 can we expect?
2. Is it preferable to teach reading in L2 first or L1 first, or both from the beginning?
3. Should we keep the L1 and L2 separate when teaching?
4. What is the importance of oral language for L2 reading competence?

Based on the research demonstrating that language immersion education (L2 literacy) doesn't diminish the learner's literacy skills in L1, Genesee advocates for greater, concentrated exposure to the L2 as early in the program as possible. Literacy skills transfer from one language to the next, particularly in languages with similar alphabet characters. Once a reader learns reading fluency skills in one language that they speak, they apply that literacy understanding to another

---

[32] In this context, a second language that is learned in school.

related language. If your English teacher teaches that you can blend letter sounds, your Portuguese teacher doesn't need to reteach that same skill. That said, he encourages teaching reading in L2 first and keeping L1 and L2 separate when teaching. Genesee cautions that elevating the status of teaching reading in L1 risks reducing L2 reading competency and related academic access in higher grades.

Proficiency levels in L1 and L2 vary depending on the structure of the immersion program. Language immersion educators often fall prey to the myth of the "perfect bilingual." Even with high functionality, immersion students still make grammar mistakes in both languages, and have less idiomatic language than same-age native speaker peers. Within environments where L1 and L2 language instruction are highly distinctive (two different teachers in two different spaces), constructivist instruction and cross-linguistic connections support learners in scaffolding specific concepts and vocabulary development.

According to Genesee's work, language immersion students struggle more with reading comprehension than with decoding skills. It is much more complex to diagnose reading comprehension difficulties if students have inadequate vocabulary and incomplete complex grammar. These two deficits become the biggest barriers for students to access academic language by grade five. Genesee advises that teachers explicitly teach academic language, starting in kindergarten and across all disciplines. This includes complex grammar as well as discipline-specific vocabulary. Language immersion teachers need to know, understand, and teach academic language from the early grades to give students the tools to thrive in reading comprehension, not just reading fluency. Early grade teachers, in particular, should constantly teach phonological awareness, word knowledge, content, and complex grammar to give students the specific tools they will need for reading comprehension.

ONE GOOD QUESTION WITH DR. ELIZA SOUZA LIMA: WE MUST TEACH CHILDREN TO LEARN: LANGUAGE LESSONS FROM NEUROSCIENCE (BRAZIL)

Language educators and researchers are fascinated by neurological data. We love to cite the latest research — "Have you read Bialystok's work on the bilingual brain?" — and share documentaries like *The Secret Life of the Brain* (Grubin, 2002). Because we still subscribe to the notion that "hard science" is more respected than social science, we tout scientific research that validates our pedagogical framework. So when Dr. Elvira Souza Lima opened her keynote speech at the 2015 Brazilian Immersion Conference and declared that "Pedagogy is the most important change in education," the room paused. Did she really mean that pedagogy is more important than neurological function for teaching and learning?

For the first half of her talk, Dr. Souza Lima paid homage to the research on memory and neurology by 2000 Nobel Prize recipient Eric Kandel. The auditorium full of international immersion school educators delighted to learn about synapses, long-term potentiation (LTP), and plasticity. How exactly do our brains convert short-term experiences to long-term memory to knowledge? What can we do to keep our brains learning as long as possible? We watched researchers animate the precise moment of "learning" in the human brain and marveled at the density of learning in the child's brain versus the adult's brain.

Dr. Souza Lima's talk quickly gave way to neurological implications for language learning. First, she parsed out oracy (listening and speaking) from literacy (reading and writing). Genetically, humans are programmed for oracy yet must learn literacy. Singing, melody, and repetition of natural sounds developed in Neanderthals before speech. Everyone can hum, cry, or sing, however poorly, without having explicitly learned to do so. In the first three years of life, the brain's language function is focused on listening and singing. During early childhood years, humans learn in the vocal area of our brain, which allows us to improve our brain's plasticity. Prevalent recommendations to speak, read, and sing to your infant not only support most important receptive functions that their brains are developing, but they expand their capacity to learn more later.

From ages three to six, the young brain develops twice as many synapses than an adult brain and this is the best time to begin forming long-term memories. Long-term memories developed during preschool years provide children with background knowledge necessary to acquire literacy skills. According to Dr. Souza Lima, the purpose of early language instruction (immersion or otherwise) in students ages four to six, is to further oracy and build plasticity. Plasticity is highest in children through age seven and then is extinguished by age ten. Daily exposure to music, arts, graphic arts, drawing, and imaginative play all contribute to plasticity in the young brain. These assertions reinforce play-based preschool and kindergarten curricular frameworks that focus on providing rich environments and new experiences for young learners to discover more about their world.

"It is not only what the child speaks, but what the child thinks."

- Dr. Souza Lima

Dr. Souza Lima frequently referenced Vygotsky during her talk to remind us that our work is not simply getting students to produce speech and words, but that in forming language, we are curating thoughts as well. Learning literacy, specific reading and writing skills, requires that your brain forms long-term memories. During the formative years of oracy, we can train our brains to learn new information and store it for long-term access. By age seven, at the peak of plasticity, the brain is ready to start learning discrete literacy skills. Can we begin learning literacy before the age of seven? Absolutely, and our world is full of autodidacts who have mastered reading fluency before they begin formal education. Developmentally, however, youth who begin reading at four do not significantly outperform youth who begin reading at seven.

Enter significant dissonance between neurological research about literacy learning and current US curriculum expectations. With little exception,

American schools subscribe to earlier and more aggressive academic and literacy instruction in attempts to accelerate learning outcomes. Not only is this practice counter to neurological productivity, but time spent "teaching reading" in early elementary years usurps the time that the brain could be developing plasticity. Recent research demonstrates that while they may initially outperform their peers, students who have been taught explicit literacy skills in grades K-2 tend to plateau their reading comprehension and language use after third grade (Stefanou, Howlett, and Peck, 2012). Early explicit literacy instruction may be a limitation to the young brain at peak plasticity and further delay access to deeper learning in later years.

Dr. Souza Lima's message was subtle, yet insistent that rich, daily experiences in music, creativity, arts, and imagination contribute significantly to the brain's capacity to learn over time. These activities are what teach the young brain to learn and provide ample opportunities to build capacity and plasticity. Exposing young learners to a wide variety of life experiences allow them to create scaffolds to which they can attach new information as they grow.

ONE GOOD QUESTION WITH DEANNE THOMAS: HOW DO WE CREATE OPPORTUNITIES FOR MĀORI TO GET INTO LEADERSHIP ROLES?

The first time I walked into the office at Core Education, I felt like I was at home. When I reached the entrance to their building in Wellington, there was a handwritten note on graph paper taped to the door. "Rhonda come in, we're upstairs." The note was written in a blue highlighter, and it closely resembled my best friend's handwriting. I think I texted her before I went inside to make sure there wasn't a surprise, waiting for me at the top of the stairs.

After visiting with team members in the Wellington and Christchurch offices, I had so many questions about how they operationalized their values for their internal working culture. Deanne Thomas and I scheduled a few calls for me to learn more about their organizational path and, as these calls usually go, they created space for me to learn how Deanne's family experience influenced her education leadership.

In what ways do our investments in education reveal our beliefs about the next generation's role in the world?

We believe in a bilingual, multilingual Aotearoa (New Zealand). To get there, every education service that we "sell" has to be culturally responsive. This requires education to work for every child, not just the majority. What drives me individually is an absolute need to see equity for all kids in New Zealand. We explore concepts of biculturalism, and through that, I see three ways that our investments impact the next generation of a bilingual Aotearoa.

Historically, New Zealand is underpinned by the Treaty of Waitangi in 1840s between the British Crown and Māori iwis, our indigenous groups. Within forty years of the Treaty, indigenous groups were decimated, but today we still have the document that protects our rights. For Māori, the Treaty allows us to keep our politicians, friends, and everyone around us honest! The Treaty didn't fix everything; some of our policies, practices, and legislation today are still incredibly biased and racist. A number of iwi have negotiated reparations for the sins of the past. Reparations here include money in hand, land, and other benefits with the intent of giving iwis a way to maintain their own agency of how they protect their language and culture.

At work we've adopted the bicultural vision from the Treaty of Waitangi, including equity, honorable governance, and self-determination. This requires unpacking. When we think about the power of the bicultural vision, the physical numbers are stacked against Māori. In our country, Māori people represent about 16% of the population and only half of us who identify as Māori, speak our language. About 11% of schools have te reo *Māori* medium instruction, including *kura kaupapa Māori*, a single immersion classroom within English medium schools. This means that less than 5% of students are taking their studies in *te reo Māori* — everyone else is learning their classes in English. One bright spot is there are a few relatively new secondary schools that teach every subject in *te reo Māori*. This has been hugely successful. They take students who don't necessarily have *te reo Māori* background, but they catch them up and students are able to speak our language at differing levels. In addition, they have the highest secondary school results in the country!

We also invest a lot of time and energy in developing published products intended for *te reo maori* speaking children in immersion schools. All the publishing companies will tell us that there's no money to be made in Māori medium publications because it's a very small market. We make our money back off of the bigger products in English. Producing English-medium products allows us to carry the cost of developing similar products for Māori-medium instruction and meet needs that have not been met in these schools for a long, long time. Now we're fortunate to have Tuia Publishing that focuses exclusively on Māori-medium books.

Our biggest investment is in culturally responsive practices to help teachers walk in other people's shoes. Teachers who know and deeply understand our students' experiences are the answer to the success in these schools. Since less than 5% of Māori youth are in *te reo Māori*-medium schools, it's the Māori students in English-medium schools who are confronted every day with teachers from a different culture. Māori students in English-medium schools have to navigate that English dominant pedagogy, so we invest support in getting English-medium teachers to become more culturally responsive for their Māori students.

In the United States, there's a lot of debate about how "proficient" you have to be in your own language to raise your children to be bilingual, and with that, a lot of shame that we speak "broken" versions of our minoritized languages. How have you navigated that?

My mother was Māori and my parents spoke Māori and English. In my generation, we grew up in a time with anti-Māori sentiment, so my parents raised all seventeen of us not to speak Māori. I married a *pakeha* guy who had immigrated to New Zealand directly from England. My young adult years overlapped with our postcolonial environment at a time when Māori people were trying to reclaim what we didn't have. Many *te reo Māori* speakers in the current generation have a huge impact on contemporary culture. I learned Māori in university. I was a career mom, and it just happened that when my children were young, the country created *kura kaupapa maori*, a total immersion preschool taught in *te reo Māori*. I would drop my kids off in the morning and they would be learning more *te reo Māori* than I knew! So I decided that I needed to learn about the language with my children. I'm still a language learner today and my goal is to share that story with as many people as possible.

In our organization, there is a very small space where adults can speak *te reo Māori* to each other. The dominant working language is English, and the dominant working viewpoint is English. I struggle with constantly looking for the Māori voice in all of our decision-making, our practices, and the ways that we support non-Māori staff in their work with Māori kids in English medium schools. In many ways, this feels like being the sole Māori teacher in a big secondary school. The difference is that some of my colleagues are getting quite proactive. They have a shared understanding that something has to change. The adoption of the Treaty is our partnership, and the outcome is *pakeha* leaders saying, "Wait, that's not what equity looks like. How are we going to address that?" And then they work toward Māori people having a voice in everything we do. Before we can be effective with bringing English-medium teachers into culturally responsive practices, we've got to be able to walk our talk and model what we say.

We expect our *pakeha* staff to examine their own bicultural and bilingual practices. Our staff have all participated in an overnight *marae* community event to see the depth of Māori culture working. *Pakeha* staff have opportunities to learn *te reo Māori* as part of their professional growth plans. When you come to our office, you hear people of all shades saying, "*Kia ora*, mates." They seek opportunities in public forums to use the language that they're learning. We have a staff *karakia* and *waiata* that everyone learns. In Māori culture, when you take a speaker out to a public forum, you support him by a song, the *waiata*. We explained this in our company and the impact when someone keeps their mouth closed during the *karakia* or *waiata*. For us it signals that you don't know the meaning of it, you don't feel comfortable with *te reo Māori*, and you don't believe in Māori cultural practices. We've moved to a space now when no one bats an eyelid when I speak *te reo Māori*. They sit and wait until someone translates or I explain. That is hugely exciting for me!

DEANNE'S ONE GOOD QUESTION: "How do we create opportunities for Māori to get into leadership roles? How can we make sure that Māori are in a position to grow, develop, and lead as everyone else?

WHAT ARE YOU WONDERING?

KAREN WONDERS: How can a student's experience build on his/her fount of knowledge, both linguistic and cultural?

DEANNE WONDERS: How do we create opportunities for Māori to get into leadership roles? How can we make sure that Māori are in a position to grow, develop, and lead as everyone else?

When you think about the right to access education in your language, who do you think deserves that right? What did you think you already knew about multilingual education access that was challenged here?

As you reflect on your one good question —

- Think about your audience: Which voices were missing from this chapter? Who are the experts for your wondering?
- Think about your context: Which languages have been systematically minoritized in your local community?
- Think about your timing: Are you trying to get clarity on what has occurred or on what could be?

WHO STILL NEEDS TO GO TO COLLEGE? COLLEGE OR NAH?

CHAPTER 6

Y PARENTS HAD ME when they were undergraduates at University of Louisiana at Lafayette. They both took breaks from school to work full time when I was young. Daddy completed his degree when I was in first grade. I still remember going to his graduation at Blackham Coliseum and then dinner at a fancy restaurant where we presented his gift — a brown leather briefcase with his initials. My mother returned to school as well but has not yet completed a degree. It's still one of the biggest regrets in her life. For my siblings and me, completing college was never a question. We've all had different experiences in school: my brother went to an HBCU[33], my sister was a scholar-athlete and an active member of Alpha Kappa Alpha Sorority, Inc., and I studied abroad in France and Cameroon.

My children have been exploring their college options and trajectories since elementary school. For years, my son thought he would be an English professor. He would periodically ask how long it took to get a PhD in English. He was mentally calculating how many more years of school it would take to achieve his dream. Both of my kids appreciate the idea of taking a gap year in between high school and university, and I wouldn't be surprised if one, or both, of them went abroad for their degree studies. My stated goal for them has always been that they have the preparation for, and perspective to pursue, multiple paths

---

[33] Historically Black Colleges and Universities.

and make real choices about what they want to do after high school. So far, they are both still assuming that university studies will be a part of that. I'm secretly relieved. Intellectually, I affirm that there can be multiple paths to a career, but emotionally, some part of me still holds onto this expectation that completing a college degree is the most important step towards the career of choice.

As a Black mother, conversations about who *should* go to college make me nervous. Black communities in the United States have been fighting for equal access to education for generations. Should we stop now? Are educators creating alternatives for lower income Black and Brown families to keep them in cycles of poverty? Are my white, middle class counterparts encouraging their children to eschew university studies? Or are college alternatives a great idea for someone else's kids?

In this chapter, we'll hear from leaders who believe that we shouldn't be pushing every student to university studies, that we should create more space for alternatives to the four-year degree.[34] One of the biggest arguments for alternative paths to career is an economic one. The cost of university in the United States has at least doubled from the 1980s to 2020s. The US has the second highest average tuition for public universities in the world[35]. Average student loan debt for a bachelor's degree is upwards of $35,000.[36] First generation university students who begin their studies, assume the debt, but do not complete a degree are too often underemployed and struggle to repay student loans.

Spoiler alert: I have some strong feelings about the cost of college in the US. In an essay that I wrote for The Future of Universities, North American Edition[37]. I shared,

> "In the United States, we've been selling university as access to the middle class for generations. It hasn't worked. African Americans with

---

[34] In the US, the four-year degree represents the bachelor's level, standard course of study at university. Some universities, community colleges, and technical colleges also offer two-year degrees or specialty certificates.

[35] OCDE (2020), *Education at a Glance 2020 : OECD Indicators*, Éditions OCDE, Paris, https://doi.org/10.1787/69096873-en.

[36] Ma, Jennifer and Matea Pender (2021). Trends in College Pricing and Student Aid 2021, New York: College Board.

[37] Broussard, Rhonda. "Towards a Liberatory University Experience." *The Future of Universities Thoughtbook: North American Edition*, edited by Meerman, A. et. al., University Industry Innovation Network, 2019, 92-94.

university degrees have less wealth than white Americans with high school diplomas. The high cost of college compounded with the burden of student loan debt is furthering the economic divide in our country. For the university of the future to meet the most challenging demands in education, it needs to be free and designed to increase belonging for all students. When universities in the United States are free — economically, pedagogically, and culturally — they will unlock our true potential as learners and creators."

- Rhonda Broussard

In this chapter we hear from Ben Nelson (USA) and Susanna Williams (USA) who both explore the social status of college and what happens if we divorce learning from name brand institutions. J.B. Schramm (USA) and Marcelo Knoebel (Brazil) question the post-secondary paradox — more jobs will require degrees, but fewer youth from low-income communities are getting them.

ONE GOOD QUESTION WITH BEN NELSON: DO WE ACTUALLY BELIEVE THAT COLLEGE MATTERS? (USA)

The first time that I heard of Minerva Schools was in conversation with Kriste Dragon, a friend whose children are a few years older than mine. We were talking about university and the tension between the guidance we received about going to college and the guidance we wanted to give our children. On the one hand, I knew that I wanted my children to have many options after high school — gap year, internship, university in the US or abroad. I also knew that I didn't want my children to be saddled with oppressive student loans for undergraduate studies. When I shared my concern about the cost of university in the US and researching less expensive options for university abroad, Kriste told me about Minerva Schools. Minerva is a highly competitive university where students study in different countries throughout their undergraduate degree. By avoiding the trappings of a well-appointed campus, Minerva is able to offer a rigorous program of study at a fraction of the cost of most private liberal arts colleges.

A couple of years later, I crossed paths with Ben Nelson, founder of Minerva Schools, at the United World College Congress in 2016. Graduates of international schools, like those at United World College, were the target population for Minerva — young people who already had some level of comfort and interest in studying in an international context. When Ben and I connected for the interview, I had lots of questions about how Minerva worked, mostly out of my parental curiosity. This book is full of educators who raise concerns about traditional instructional models, but Ben is perhaps the only one whose hypothesis challenges the perceived status of educational institutions, pedagogy, and economics.

In what ways do our investments in education reveal our beliefs about the next generation's role in the world?

Education matters. It sounds so banal and simple. Everyone in the world says this, but I argue that no one actually believes that education matters. Here's proof:

Imagine a high school student who has the option to go to A) Harvard or B) some other less prestigious educational institution where they will get a better education. How many people are going to say don't go to Harvard? Effectively nobody.

If people actually believed that education mattered, then college rankings, curricula, and choice wouldn't exist in these formats. Fundamentally, no one believes that education matters, but that the credentials do. People think, "have credentials, will travel." And they're wrong. Credentials don't really matter. Credentials are ultimately put to the test when you get to the real world.

The investment —whether it is in dollars, human capital, time and money — that yields the most returns in your life is learning. It's not getting an education.

You're shifting the whole paradigm here – learning matters but learning institutions less so? I still believe in "school," so help me understand this.

We need to make a distinction between getting an education, being educated and actually learning. One of the key elements to know that learning has occurred is the concept called "far transfer." Far transfer occurs when people apply learning from one context to a problem/need in a radically different context. You know that someone has learned when they say, "I've never seen this before, but I've seen all of these common elements. I studied XYZ and there are patterns developed between them that I recognize here. With certainty, I know that if I do ABC, I will likely get positive results."

So for families wondering where to invest in their children's success, invest in education, not the credential.

How do you get people to shift their values towards "education" not credential?

"Hyperbolic discounting" is the phenomenon that things get better with age. Among youth and adults, if you are told "you can invest $10 today and get $100 five years from now," most people say they would rather spend the $10 today. Similarly, when you tell an 18-year-old kid you shouldn't drop acid/do coke because though you're going to have a lot of fun tonight, you may ruin your life ten years from now, they discount it. Thinking about short-term reward versus long-term benefit is built into human nature.

It's hard to admit that you don't believe in our education system. When push comes to shove and you're at the supermarket, run into your old friend, and she asks where your kid is going to school, you'd want to say Harvard (or whichever university has status for you). You don't want to say she's getting an amazing education at an "unbranded institution." You sacrifice the future well-being of your child to have an easier supermarket conversation. That's how human beings behave.

How do we have a republic that works? People understand and are informed instead of responding to their cognitive biases. They commit to spending the time thinking about how not to generate irrational biases. That requires long-term thinking, i.e., I'm going to spend more time pouring through this article, so that my one vote will be a beacon of light and influence others. We're not built to think that way even though we live in a world that requires us to. That's the problem we're stuck in. We're not designed for the modern world. We're still designed to be hunters and gatherers. The only solution I see to our problem is long-term and systemic. Minerva Schools at KGI exist to reform education systems all over the world. We believe that reform occurs when the most prestigious institutions reset and cause a ripple effect to go through the rest of the system. Education reform is a process that will take longer than my lifetime.

Don't divorce the 2016 US Presidential election outcomes from what government policy has been over the past several decades. Republicans and Democrats have focused fifty years of higher education policy on increasing access, increasing completion, and more recently, lowering costs. The easiest way to increase college access, college completion, and make it cheaper is to lower standards. It's the easiest way. Anyone can go, anyone can finish, and it'll be cheaper.

If you actually educate your citizens, and not just drive people towards the same credentials, more of the population will be ready to take the next step. When you apply the science of learning, students are more engaged and are ready to make informed choices. Completion rates then increase.

Thirdly, as education institutions focus on education, they can shed all of the outrageous cost levels that universities are currently in the trap of doing: sports, research salaries, campus museums, and performing arts centers. The cost burden of creating these "country clubs" falls to students and taxpayers but what's the return on investment? If higher ed actually focused on education, then we could solve this. College access and completion rates are only symptoms of a poorly functioning education system. You have to treat the root cause.

> **BEN'S ONE GOOD QUESTION:** "How do you enable wise decision-making in a world with unwise people?

ONE GOOD QUESTION WITH SUSANNA WILLIAMS: IS HIGHER ED THE EQUALIZER WE THINK? (USA)

If you've ever met her, you know that Susanna Williams is a talker. I can't recall our first conversation, though I think we went from a random comment to a deep analysis about leadership development within minutes. Among the many things that Susanna does professionally, she is passionate about alternate routes to career access. Susanna has developed competency-based training and development programs and registered apprenticeship programs for businesses and higher education institutions around the country. What I appreciate about this interview is how Susanna centers community colleges when discussing access to employment, perceived status, and skill development.

In what ways do our investments in education reveal our beliefs about the next generation's role in the world?

Higher education has seen wholesale disinvestment since 2008. The majority of students in our country attend public universities, and 26% attend community colleges. Liberal arts and research institutions serve a very small population of US students, and their funding challenges are unique. As the economy has recovered since 2008, the funding has not returned to state-funded higher education. Part of this is a function of discretionary spending at the state level because very little funding comes from the federal government. Most states have mandated spending that has to be accounted for, but higher education is one of the few discretionary lines, so states tend to turn to the public universities and say "charge more tuition." At the same time tuition is increasing, we're getting the message that the full pathway to life is through earning a college degree. Universities are then seeking outside students — foreign nationals and out-of-state students — who will pay the sticker price for tuition as opposed to the in-state rates. This results in state universities having fewer seats available for lower-income applicants.

Employers then use the college name as a basis for hiring. So, community college students are at a disadvantage on the hiring market, unless they are health care assistants, and the hospital has a relationship with their specific college program. Connections become pathways to employment and prosperity. When we do not fund quality education yet hold people's lives accountable as though they have received that education, we're actually saying that we don't believe that education is something that everyone in our country should have equal access to. Society is saying that we're okay with some people being poor and we're okay with some people not having access to opportunity.

How did the funding become discretionary? Higher education and public policy have not caught up with modern times. When state constitutions were written, basic education was just K-12 through the 1970s. At that time, you could get a great manufacturing job or vocational training and make solid money with a K-12 education. Then the world changed. The only thing slower to change than education is the government. There is a strong case for community colleges to be a part of basic education and should be included as K-14 education. The state of Washington's constitution's first priority is to fully fund basic education, but they're not meeting basic expectations. Look at public school funding formulas. They are driven by property taxes and tax code and no one wants to tackle the tax code. It's not sexy and doesn't win you elections.

Who's actually having this conversation? I'm not sure people are connecting the dots. The only way it's happening is through lawsuits over K-12 education. State legislatures have been held in contempt of court because they haven't figured out equitable funding for schools. What we need to be talking about is what families do to subsidize public education. We need to be asking what does it actually cost to educate a child who does not grow up with the benefit of a house with books, afterschool curriculum, or a print-rich nursery school environment? What does a middle-class child have as ancillary benefits? What are the habits that their families inculcate and the culture that they grow up in? How can we provide those standards for all children?

In our analog/digital divide, higher ed institutions are working feverishly to incorporate new tech tools and communication paradigms into their pedagogy and engagement. Do the tools really matter for this generation? How should post-secondary institutions position themselves for responsive and inclusive engagement?

Many higher education institutions in Europe have parochial roots and often their primary function was to train priests. Higher education today retains the vestiges of that holy process. It is serious and magical and spiritual, and you can't touch that or dirty that with technology and money is the worst kind of profanity. People keep calling for the end of college. Colorado had a major freak-out about MOOCs (Massive Open Online Courses), which challenge the delivery of higher education. I think there's a big disruption coming. Competency-based education is going to shift the paradigm and project-based learning will change instructional practice. Badges of proficiency will change that option. When we remove the Carnegie credit hour and let students show what they can do, then we no longer need to have institutions as arbiters of confidence.

We say that institution and pedigree matter, yet people still hire based on who they know and how comfortable they feel with that person. Take the example of the HBO series *The Wire* and the network of the drug dealers on the street. That show demonstrates that networks are equally powerful in both informal economy and formal economy. Our challenge is to figure out how to teach and give networks to other people. If you win the school lottery and leave East Flatbush, New York, and make it to an Ivy League institution, there's no guarantee that you will be able to access the network of the Ivy League. This example assumes that access and equity are goals of education. There's a big divide in education philosophy between those who are warriors for justice through education and those who are gatekeepers to keep marginalized people out of power structures. I forget that others use education as a sorting tool.

> **SUSANNA'S ONE GOOD QUESTION:** "How do we effectively move people to opportunity in our country, if we don't agree that everyone should have opportunity?

IS COLLEGE STILL RELEVANT? ONE GOOD QUESTION WITH J.B. SCHRAMM (USA)

In this chapter, we hear from educators, who, frustrated with traditional college expectations, created their own alternative college model or advocate for community college pathways. They want college to work better for young people. J.B. Schramm enters the conversation from a different starting point. He built his career in college access programming to support young people through the college interest, application, and persistence processes. When J.B. started his first nonprofit in his basement in 1995, he was inspired by youth agency and influence to make college relevant in peer circles of students who were often the first generation in their family to attend university. In this interview, he brings the perspective of youth influence and youth voice into his analysis about college.

In what ways do our investments in education reveal our beliefs about the next generation's role in the world?

Every school success paradigm I've seen involves similar components: excellent educators, school leaders, data and measurement, standards, etc., but what you never see is "students" as part of the solution. We have this sense that students are vessels into which education is to be poured. In order to move forward in our communities, we need young people from our communities to take charge. They need to have confidence and be equipped as critical thinkers, problem solvers, strategists, and risk takers. They need the motivation to challenge power structures and be problem solvers in the broader community. We don't win, and our nation doesn't become a more just place, simply by informing students. We need to offer them the responsibility to take charge of their education and future.

The fact is young people are most influenced by their peers. Young people today are taking responsibility for more and more parts of their lives, either because adults are abnegating obligations, or because technology is giving youth more opportunity to control their own communication and networks.

Young people influence young people tremendously. We are missing a huge opportunity when we define students as the objects of education. The key that we need in our investments is to show that young people can be drivers of their education. They can take charge of improving achievement in their schools. The paradigm changes when you start with the premise that the young people are on your side, that they can be driving education gains not only for themselves but also for their classmates.

I learned these lessons working at College Summit, a US nonprofit championing student-driven college success. College Summit coined the phrase #PeerForward, which means to find and train a community's most influential students in college access and leadership so that they run campaigns with their peers to file FAFSA, apply to college, and explore careers. In this model, the peers are owning the outcomes, not just following adult voice. That's a very powerful model. We all care more when we own something. When you're talking about under-resourced institutions, the most powerful resource that schools need is already there in abundance — the students!! They can solve their problems. They want to achieve, and they want to be challenged. For teenagers, especially just when they are hungry for greater challenges, we so often keep them in the same sort of structure as elementary school. Let's take off the training wheels and give them the chance to take on bigger challenges.

Given all of the contemporary discourse about the ways that traditional K-12 education is not preparing students for the new global economy, is college still relevant?

In 2014, I co-authored a white paper with Andy Rotherham and Chad Aldeman that outlines today's post-secondary paradox. On the one hand, college is more valuable than ever. In the immediate term the wage premium is about 70%, the highest it's ever been. From a medium-term perspective, the number of jobs requiring postsecondary education is climbing. Today, just 45% of Americans have a post-secondary degree, and by 2025, 65% of jobs will require one. If you want to be in the running for that set of jobs, education beyond high school is essential[38].

---

[38] For more information, see Lumina Foundation's A Stronger Nation report and online tools: https://www.luminafoundation.org/stronger-nation/report

At the same time, college is riskier than ever with historic debt loads, and employers questioning the value of many postsecondary programs.

So how can students handle the post-secondary paradox? Young people need to be smart shoppers about their post-secondary education. You can no longer blindly get a degree from anywhere. Some colleges do a much better job of educating and graduating students than others; plus, students need to navigate a wider array of options for quality postsecondary education today. You can no longer meander across majors, without considering career goals. That's not to say students should lock into a career path in ninth grade. Teens are not going to all of a sudden know what they will want to do in twenty years; data suggests that they change jobs even more frequently than previous generations. Students benefit when they consider careers that interest them, and the economic potential of those fields, and then thoughtfully explore them.

As smart shoppers, students can consider which range of careers intrigue them, which postsecondary programs will get them on the right path, and which institutions most effectively graduate students from similar backgrounds. The postsecondary paradox leaves students more in need of college-going know-how than ever before. Unfortunately, due to budget constraints, school districts are dedicating fewer and fewer resources for college and career planning. Not surprisingly, college-going rates are down, especially for low-income students.

Students, parents, and community organizations need to step up, help schools prioritize college and career planning, and access the resources — including influential students, recent college grads, and volunteer mentors who are close at hand. Check out programs like College Advising Corps, College Possible, and iMentor that are already doing this.

The need for postsecondary education, and in fact deeper postsecondary education, becomes more pronounced the farther out we look. Some labor theorists predict we're on the verge of the greatest workforce shift since the Industrial Revolution. Over the next few decades, large employment sectors will disappear, they say, due to automation, robotics, artificial intelligence, etc. How can we prepare for a world like that? I think we need to be skeptical of hyper-focusing on training students for what the job market requires right now. Narrowly directing students to fill today's job gaps may lead to employment and aid certain industries in the short term, but it's not in the service of our kids, nation, or industry in the long term. Rather, we need to raise the conversation about the future of work with students, employers, education innovators, and technologists. Also, I believe it's a smart bet that this brave new world will favor people who can lead, create, problem solve, work in teams, and persevere. At College Summit, they call those attributes Power Skills. These are the skills employers cite today as being most in demand. The most effective colleges develop Power Skills well, as do challenging work experiences, and demanding community service work. For example, we have seen Power Skills develop in College Summit Peer Leaders running peer campaigns in their high schools. For America to prosper relative to advancing economies around the world, we need to develop this kind of deeper learning in all students, in every corner of our nation. The question isn't "whether" young people should get a postsecondary education, it's which kind of postsecondary education? Now is not the moment to soften ambitions, especially for students from low-income and underrepresented communities climbing uphill. Nor is it time to resign ourselves to status quo postsecondary education. We need to challenge our students, educators, employers, and technologists to stretch, figuring out better ways for students to learn and take charge of their future.

> **J.B.'S ONE GOOD QUESTION:** How can young people drive their education and improve student achievement in their communities?

ONE GOOD QUESTION WITH MARCELO KNOBEL: GENERAL STUDIES REFORM FOR BRAZIL'S UNIVERSITIES (BRAZIL)

There is a Chinese proverb that says, "If you want to know what water is, don't ask a fish." The idea is that the fish's conditions are so normal for them, they wouldn't even be able to describe their atmosphere. When I spoke with Marcelo Knobel, I realized how much I had normalized the American model of a liberal arts education. I did my undergraduate studies at Washington University in St. Louis because I wanted a degree program that could lead me to a professional certificate and afford me the space to explore different and at times, disparate, courses of study outside of my major. I knew that in my second year of studies, I would declare a major in education that included preparation for teacher certification.

When I started university, I really thought I would become an early childhood educator. After just one year working with preschoolers in an afterschool program, I changed my focus to secondary education. After all, I had worked and volunteered with middle schoolers since I was seventeen, so it felt like the right age group for me. When I planned my study abroad program in Cameroon, that inadvertently solidified my path to a degree in secondary education and a certification as a French language teacher. I had been very interested in literacy and language acquisition in English but studying abroad meant that it would take me five years to complete my degree. I didn't want the added expense or time and made a decision that allowed me to study in Cameroon and still complete my degree as planned. A liberal arts education afforded me the space to explore, reflect, and revise my path in the same university without additional applications, fees, or delays. Until I met Marcelo, I thought this was normal.

Marcelo is a physicist by training who would not have imagined himself as an education advocate. He has written hundreds of scholarly publications and served as Executive Director of the Brazilian National Nanotechnology Laboratory (LNNano), Brazilian Center for Research in Energy and Materials (CNPEM). But when he was a professor at UNICAMP, he was inspired to ask different questions on behalf of his students.

In what ways do our investments in education reveal our beliefs about the next generation's role in the world?

Sometimes there is an investment in education, but the priorities are completely wrong. In Brazil we have significant investments — the government pays for K-12 and university education for all students, but the priorities are not leading us to strong education outcomes. Our system and needs are really complex, but there are two existing investments that could be better leveraged for change: value of the teacher as a professional and scalability of non-governmental education organizations. Our teachers are underpaid and not well-prepared for the work, and society provides no incentive to be a professor, or positive value of the profession. To change that, for the next generation, it's necessary to have a really smart and fast plan to change this situation. This is where the scalability of non-governmental organizations matters. There are philanthropic and social investment efforts here, but they aren't as well developed as in the US. It's difficult to keep a non-governmental organization (ONG) running. There are a few ONGs run by civil society or wealthy families, but their impact is very small in comparison to the need. Fundaçao Lemann is making some interesting programs, but the number of people that these programs can impact is small. Brazil should have 1,000 organizations like Fundaçao Lemann, but we may have only ten. Scaling the impact of our ONGs would reach a much broader population than we can do currently.

In your upcoming book, you posit that Brazilian higher education would benefit from offering general liberal arts colleges among existing post-secondary institutions. What void will liberal arts colleges fill and how will they transform access and success for the greater population?

My main concern is to advocate for the cause of general education in university. In Brazil, 43% of the population completes high school on average, but only 12%

has a post-secondary degree[39], so we're already dealing with an elite population. The benefits for these elites are very clear — better salaries, better jobs. In our university system, we currently have no general education or liberal arts course requirements. When a student tests to enter university, they are only applying to a specific career strand: medicine, education, chemistry, accounting, etc. It may seem like a minor detail but it's not. Some careers are extremely difficult to access. At UNICAMP for example, less than 1% of applicants are accepted into the medical program. If you are accepted and after one month you don't like this course of study, you have to drop-out of university and start all over for the next year. A general studies or liberal arts base would allow students to experiment and learn more about specific industries before making a commitment to one of them.

In the real world when companies hire engineers, they provide a six-month training period for the specific content in that position. The ideal candidates are excellent learners and problem-solvers first, then content experts. Usually, companies prefer to hire people who can think outside of the box and have certain soft skills that we don't learn here in Brazil at all. General education has been in place in the US for years. In the global market, companies and countries like China, Singapore, and Hong Kong are in search of more well-rounded professionals who can deal with problems and learn how to solve them across multiple disciplines. If you're only learning content in university, within ten years your content may be outdated.

ProFIS created at UNICAMP is a hybrid of my general education vision. This is a pilot that I would like to see the entire university adopt. We recruit the best students from the local public high school, who wouldn't normally attend university. On average 80% of students are living in poverty and 90% are first generation in the university. We're automatically increasing social inclusion by making a space for these students in university.

Even when these students are the best in their schools, they still have strong gaps in their basic education. ProFIS anticipates and supports academic and socioeconomic gaps with an army of staff and resources: the best professors in university volunteer to teach in ProFIS, teaching assistants provide extra tutoring, social workers help with problems at home — if students don't show up for one week, we call the home to get them back, and we pay students a

---

[39] BRAZIL – Country Note – Education at a Glance 2013: OECD Indicators.

minimum wage to prevent them from dropping out because they need to earn money for their family. Fifty percent of our students continue on to traditional university studies.

The problem is that ProFIS is only a tiny drop in the bucket. We can only admit 120 students per class (about 10% of applicants), but we have thousands who have this need. If this program could be replicated in 100 universities, it could start making a difference. We need advocacy with the university system, the legislature, and large employers. If employers are clamoring for this particular employee profile with a well-rounded education, then our country will make changes. Politicians need to advocate the change. Universities need to replicate. We also need to educate the general population to know that this can exist so that they can demand it. My upcoming book will show how this is possible and trending all over the world. Brazil is out of alignment with this trend, and we should make a difference to catch up.

MARCELO'S ONE GOOD QUESTION: Is it possible for my children to have a better future? Thinking about global warming, economic depression, and education — will they even have any place to go?

WHAT ARE YOU WONDERING?

BEN WONDERS: How do you enable wise decision-making in a world with unwise people?

SUSANNA WONDERS: How do we effectively move people to opportunity in our country, if we don't agree that everyone should have opportunity?

J.B. WONDERS: How can young people drive their education and improve student achievement in their communities?

MARCELO WONDERS: Is it possible for my children to have a better future? Thinking about global warming, economic depression, and education, will they even have any place to go?

When you think about who goes to college and who benefits the most from college, what comes to mind? What did you already know about college outcomes that was challenged by the perspectives in this chapter?

As you reflect on your one good question —

- Think about your audience: Which voices were missing from this chapter? Who are the experts for your wondering?
- Think about your context: Education 2030 names gender parity as a consistent need in post-secondary education access. How is gender impacting postsecondary access and attainment in your community? When you consider how gender intersects with race or nationality, residency, socioeconomic status, and documentation status, who is most marginalized from post-secondary education?
- Think about your timing: Are you trying to get clarity on what has occurred or on what could be?

THE YEAR IN REVIEW: 10 GOOD QUESTIONS

Asking the right questions is more important than having the right answers. One of my favorite parts of these interviews was to hear these amazingly accomplished, visionary thinkers and doers ask questions that they couldn't answer on their own. I'm looking forward to hearing more good questions in the future.

---

1. Zaki's One Good Question: Education is about creating global peace. Are we matching what we really want to accomplish through education? Are we missing the way that education should be defined? (Bangladesh)

---

2. Saku's One Good Question: My question is an extremely boring one: What is the point of school? Once we answer that, then we can move on to the question of how to educate all youth. (Finland)

---

3. Michael's One Good Question: How much input should local, state, and federal governments have on the programmatic strategies of schools, given their variation in education goals and knowledge of effective programs ? (United States)

---

4. Noelle's One Good Question: How well does our education system in Malaysia engage boys? (Malaysia)

---

5. Allan's One Good Question: Given the importance that we place on education and that we know what it takes to provide high quality education for all children, why haven't we solved it for all children? That's what this country has to wrestle with. (United States)

---

6. **Alex's One Good Question:** As a parent, I value personalization, socio-emotional development, and self-directed learning a lot more than I did as an educator. What do those seemingly disparate perspectives mean about high quality education for all children? (United States)

---

7. **Marcelo's One Good Question:** Is it possible for my children to have a better future? Thinking about global warming, economic depression, and education, will they even have any place to go? (Brazil)

---

8. **Karen's One Good Question:** How can a student's experience build on his/her fount of knowledge, both linguistic and cultural ? (United States)

---

9. **Ellen's One Good Question:** If the most critical student competencies for the future are about addressing complex problems with diverse populations, how can we better prepare teachers to do the same? (United States)

And the one that got us all started,

10. **Rhonda's One Good Question:** In what ways do our investments in education reveal our beliefs about the next generation's role in the world? (United States)

What good questions will you ask about our world's education needs?

DO STUDENTS HAVE THE RIGHT TO AGENCY IN THEIR OWN EDUCATION?

CHAPTER 7

CONSIDER THAT I'm writing this introduction during the week that my twelve-year-old has started a new school, in the middle of the school year, and in the middle of the COVID-19 pandemic. Yesterday, he came home elated and, unsolicited, said, "I love my new school." As a lifelong public-school student and educator, I felt a lot of guilt about transitioning my son from one of the most highly regarded public schools in our community, to a private micro school. I thought that my professional reputation would be questioned if I revealed that the traditional public school model was not working for my son.

The irony is that, a few years ago, I gave a talk about how some micro schools provided more opportunities for youth agency, youth voice, and shared power in the learning environment. Depending on the model, a micro school has the potential to eliminate some of the hierarchy and status quo that traditional schools embody. Intellectually, I believe that youth voice matters in formal and informal education settings. So when my son came to me and said he wanted to go to a different type of school, it should have been easy for me to hear right? How could I have been a dogged advocate for student voice as an education administrator, but still question the voice of my own child? As adults, whether on the parenting side or the education leadership side, we sometimes get entrenched in our position. After all, we, as parents have successfully navigated school, we've earned the degrees, we've received the training and the accolades (the accolades!), shouldn't our kids or our students' parents or our teachers just trust what we're doing?

I sit on the Board of Directors of a different micro school that follows the Agile Learning Center (ALC) model. Agile Learning Centers are deeply rooted in student agency for learners of all ages. There is no established curriculum, no adult assessment of or reporting on student learning, and no assigned courses or coursework. The ALC community believes in self-directed learning which, for their schools, means that:

> "Humans are natural learners. When children get to follow their passions, they engage deeply, learning more quickly and thoroughly – covering years of content in weeks at the time they choose to learn it."[40]

A few years ago, I spoke on a panel titled "Wakanda Forever: Si Se Puede, Imagining a Decolonized Education System." During this conversation, my colleagues and I discussed how to eradicate white supremacy culture and the white cultural canon from our pedagogies. There were lots of nods of agreement from the Black and Brown educators in the room. When I spoke about centering student voice in our instructional practices, again the group was receptive to the idea of listening to young people. When I described the Agile Learning Center ethos to this group of education leaders, I started to lose the crowd. When the question of education oppression and power hoarding was anchored in race, class, and gender, we could exteriorize the colonial threat. When faced with considerations of age and perceived intellectual superiority, the same educators were much less interested in relinquishing some of their power. How might you be advocating for increased freedom, voice, and agency while still grappling with how your practices limit those same things for young people?

In this chapter we hear from educators who explore this paradox of agency in formal education. Susan Patrick (United States), Alex Hernandez (United States), and Nicole Young (United States) challenge us to think about student agency both in the classroom and at the policy level. Peter Howe (Canada/The Netherlands) explores how administrators can center student voice now.

---

[40] Agile Learning Centers, *agilelearningcenters.org*, Accessed March 7, 2021.

ONE GOOD QUESTION WITH SUSAN PATRICK: WHAT STUDENTS (AND SCHOOLS) CAN DO IF WE STOP RANKING THEM (USA)

All of the one good question interviews were about an hour long, but this conversation with Susan Patrick was unique because it yielded two completely different pieces. In this second piece, Susan explores her take-aways from a fellowship in New Zealand. Both Susan and I had been Eisenhower Fellows in New Zealand; however, we worked a few years apart from each other. Both of our fellowships included a focus on education and school site visits, so much of what Susan described from her observations was familiar to me. The questions that surface in this interview are more about large systemic changes. What would it look like to build different accountability systems at the school district or state level?

In what ways do our investments in education reveal our beliefs about the next generation's role in the world?

From a student-centered perspective, what are the investments being made in the learning environments? In a rapidly changing world, we need to examine the foundations of our education both for the purpose of education and its results. Are we preparing every student for the world they are entering, or are we investing in a factory model of education designed as an assembly line? The old model of education is under question and is being challenged by educators around the world with questions of appropriateness and whether it is fit for the purpose of preparing all students for success in today's world.

The investments made in today's education system are often reinforcing the basic traditional structures to grade and sort students, with limited exposure to one class at a time, one subject at a time, one textbook at a time, with one teacher at a time — with inevitable outcomes of ranking students. The premise of our society's investments in an education system that is based on sorting kids remains for the most part unchallenged. We don't examine how funding could follow the student toward ensuring equity and support to ensure every child reaches mastery of the same high standards and develops competencies for future success. The urgency of school funding debates means we need to consider what designs are better suited to ensure each and every student has access to the best educational opportunities, and make a case for investments in a transformed system, rather than tinkering with a system that sorts and ranks kids, a system designed for a world that no longer exists.

We have 13,515 school districts in the US making investments in education approaches and environments. The traditional system is based on Carnegie units and seat time, providing varying levels of learning on an A-F grading system, and whether the students have gaps or not, the clock marches on. Are these investments that we've been making for the past ten to twenty years designed to innovate and ensure student success? Are we making investments for each student to be able to have access to innovative models for equity? The investment in modernized education includes the learning spaces, but more importantly, it's the pedagogical experience for what's happening in learning.

We have been historically funding a system based on minimal exposure to subjects, with one way of approaching learning. We dictate how much "learning" might happen based on easy to manage bell schedules and calendars. The inverse system would be to realize, in a given hour of time, there might be variable amounts of learning. Thus, we need to design for supporting the maximum learning in each hour, not the minimum learning. How do we design for how kids learn best? We need to know their readiness level, existing competencies, and how to meet them where they are. If we ask about how investments reveal what we believe about education, investing in a system that ranks and sorts kids means that we are okay with this approach. I'd argue that we should invest in identifying what every student needs and ensuring the investment reflects an approach that maximizes every student's potential and future success. Right now, we're not investing in understanding where every student is when they enter school. What is their academic readiness level? What are their social and emotional, needs? How do we address the whole child and their learning experiences? Today, we're having an entire conversation in the United States about investing in summative testing as an autopsy at the end of the year instead of addressing the very needs of the students from day one.

We talk about college and career readiness as part of an important goal in our K-12 education system. Our system is designed to rank and sort kids (GPA and a class rank) to determine their college access. Is that not telling us that the system is built on an institutional fixed mindset? If we had an institutional growth mindset, we would hold the bar high for all students to learn to reach the same high outcomes. What does it take to get all students to the 4.0 GPA? This end goal would be a worthy investment for our future and our society's future.

How do we innovate our system for all students to be successful?

During my Eisenhower Fellowship in New Zealand, when I walked into every school, I could see that they were focused on meeting students where they are. When I looked around the classroom, I could see the articulation of the curriculum frameworks on the importance of twenty-first century skills, a broader definition of student success, visibility of the language of learning about rhetoric, context, thinking critically and solving complex problems. The wall posters actually had reminders to teachers: creativity and entrepreneurial thinking, communicating and collaborating, making sense through the use of knowledge, research and synthesis, understanding the information and opportunities to identify new ways of doing things. Are we asking bigger questions on what we want our students to know and be able to do? The language of learning in modern classrooms with redesigned curriculum asks the "big questions" about core concepts of learning. Whether in primary school or in secondary school, the language of learning is targeted at the appropriate level. Students from a young age are learning from a metacognitive perspective: What are the ways I am thinking about this? Am I developing skills for a changing world? How is this relevant to how I might participate and contribute to a fair and just society? They ask themselves: Am I analyzing? Am I learning how to function and self-manage? Am I learning new ways of working, new ways of thinking and skills that I will need to make sense of the world?

In some New Zealand schools, they have multi-grade classrooms and the students have clearly identified learning objectives posted across multiple levels. The teachers are constantly working with every student to identify their learning goals, assess their performance on evidence of their mastery, and co-design the next steps as students move on to the next learning objective once they've demonstrated that mastery to the level of proficiency. Each student can see what they need extra help in and can go to other students to get help. Educators in every school and classroom refer to questions like:

- How can teachers best meet students' needs?
- How can we personalize instruction?
- How can we better identify students' needs?
- Which research-based practices are most effective?
- How can we improve what's working and not working?

It was a culture of inquiry in a personalized learning environment.

David Hood, former head of New Zealand Qualifications Authority[41], has described the traditional model of K-12 as the paradigm of one: One teacher, teaching one subject, to one class, at one time, for one hour. In New Zealand, in 2007, they created a different curriculum that asked what each student needed to learn and do with a broader definition of student success. It gives a lot of flexibility to teachers and students in how they reach those goals and hold all students to the same high standards. The five key competencies are:

- Thinking
- Using language, symbols, and texts
- Managing self
- Relating to others
- Participating and contributing

Then Secretary for Education Sewell wrote, "The New Zealand Curriculum is a clear statement of what we deem important in education. It takes as its starting point a vision of our young people as lifelong learners who are confident and creative, connected, and actively involved. It includes a clear set of principles on which to base curriculum decision making. It sets out values that are to be encouraged, modeled, and explored. It defines five key competencies that

---

[41] National office that administers educational assessment and qualifications.

are critical to sustained learning and effective participation in society and that underline the emphasis on lifelong learning."[42]

We know through learning sciences that all students can learn, all students can develop a growth mindset. We actually can create learning environments that will dramatically improve outcomes and do so in a way that empowers students' own passions and interests. The education system in New Zealand includes many schools that have been designed around personalized learning and are working intently on closing the achievement gap and raising the bar for all students. The goal is that all students are not only meeting literacy and numeracy skills, but ultimately, when they graduate, they've built a whole set of knowledge, skills, competencies, and dispositions that will lead to them being contributive in society and help contribute to the free and open society. New Zealanders' cultural values are deeply reflected in their education work. Maybe that's easier to do when each school is autonomous, and the school can set their values clearly.

New Zealand schools have more local control than schools in the United States, don't they?

Absolutely! Some education systems are top down, others are bottom up in terms of their governance and control. In New Zealand, each school is autonomous and self-managed with their own principal, and each has its own elected board of trustees from the community. They set values, goals and set the accountability framework for results and metrics. How community values tie into local control is interesting. New Zealand is really a case study in empowerment of local schools and local families setting their own accountability goals. In the first school that I visited, the opening presentation was about their annual goal to reach one-and-a-half years of growth for each student. That goal had been set by the community. Everyone was on the same page, clear and transparent about that target and what they needed to do. All families have choices for the school they attend, and they choose to go to the school. It's a nice balance in New Zealand where the top-down directives from the Ministry of Education work across all schools to design a curriculum framework that will ensure a broad definition of student success and ensure the bar is the same high bar for all students. The top-down approach is simply examining the research on a world-class

---

[42] The New Zealand Curriculum, *https://nzcurriculum.tki.org.nz/The-New-Zealand-Curriculum*, Accessed March 7, 2021.

education to set that bar high to make sure the curriculum is right. The empowerment is a bottom-up approach, creating capacity for educators and practitioners to design learning activities around the research on how students learn best.

I also observed how local control impacts their governance. In the US, our unit of local elections is with the local district's school board. Anyone can run and anyone with political aspirations can be elected to the local school board (if they win the vote) as part of further political aspirations. In New Zealand, you're only eligible to run for the board of trustees of a school if you're nominated by a teacher or parent in that school community. It is an interesting approach to building community engagement and capacity.

In the discourse about preparing youth for jobs that don't yet exist, educators fall into two camps: skills-focused (STEM, design thinking, makers, etc.) and people-focused (critical thinking, global sensitivity, socio-emotional learning). To what extent are we creating a false dichotomy?

I think it's a false dichotomy. Learning is an incredibly humanistic pursuit. We're talking about helping each and every child work to their fullest potential, which is tied to relationships, understanding student interest, student goals and how to achieve them.

In the world that we live in today, if you have Wi-Fi, you can access a lot of content — it's all available to you. But what's more important is having a baseline knowledge on how content fits together and how you can approach critical thinking, creativity, problem-solving, and questioning the ideas and perspectives presented to you. That's really important in terms of being relational and contextual in the idea of people focused — how do we challenge or explore ideas effectively? Cultural responsiveness, global sensitivity, and social-emotional learning (SEL) are becoming more important than ever. Having those deep people-focused skills doesn't mean that you can't also be approaching STEM or creative design or "makers" together.

Back to New Zealand, I visited schools with more interdisciplinary approaches to learning. Students are able to identify big conceptual projects, design learning experiences that respond to community or students' needs, and then map which standards and subjects they'll be addressing in these projects.

For example, in one school, I walked over to the closest student, a fifteen-year-old boy and asked him about his project. He said he was studying Artificial Intelligence (AI) and he explained his full plan to me: he would first conduct a literature review on how AI has evolved over the past thirty years; then, he wanted to explore what trends were likely to occur in the next five years in AI; and finally, he wanted to finish the project with an analysis of the societal and ethical implications of AI in the future. He explained how he would be able to be evaluated across many of the key competencies and develop mastery of standards. He shared that he is mapping his project to the attainment of science standards, some math standards, some English/text/communication standards, and social studies standards for the ethical implications. I was amazed by the variety of ways he was able to build an understanding of the world, and at the same time articulate how he was attaining competencies and credits for his qualifications toward a degree. That's a great example of how an education system can be both skills-focused and people-focused with interdisciplinary approaches using multiple perspectives to contribute to deeper learning — that is highly personalized for each student.

Even in their elementary schools, I witnessed New Zealand's teachers asking students to take on big questions and build the capacity for learning in their own classrooms. This means really giving students agency and empowerment with the language around learning through analysis, perspective, and ethics. It was really amazing how young students were very focused on knowledge and the range of skills that they were developing. As David Hood noted, "Literacy and numeracy do include the ability to use language, symbols and texts; but these are only tools — it is the ability to use these interactively, in a connected way in context, that the OECD identifies as most important, as it does in being able to use both knowledge and information, and technology, in interactive ways." Teachers were trying to not only give students the language, tools, and strategies to address academic issues, but the strategies that would help them solve more complex problems and ultimately be successful in college, career, societies, and their communities.

> **SUSAN'S ONE GOOD QUESTION:** Will we be investing in the capabilities of thinking critically and creatively, and problem solving with the deep cultural responsiveness we will need to navigate an increasingly changing world?

ONE GOOD QUESTION WITH ALEX HERNANDEZ: PERSONALIZED LEARNING AND DESIGN THINKING MATTER FOR ALL KIDS (USA)

When Alex Hernandez and I spoke for this interview, he was leading an education investment portfolio. He leveraged his prior experience as a teacher, building administrator, and regional superintendent to, by his own definition, spend his days being intensely curious about instructional models and innovation in the classroom. His twins and my daughter are about the same age, so any time we talked about schools, the conversation always touched on this triangle: what are we advocating for as educators, what do we want for our own kids as parents, and what are our kids telling us they need in their learning environment? These three questions rarely yielded the same bright ideas. Many of the educators in this book are focused on large scale systems change and, during this slice of his professional career, Alex was more focused on micro solutions.

In what ways do our investments in education reveal our beliefs about the next generation's role in the world?

I see two big trends that guide how I think about investing philanthropy.

First, we are in a generational change towards school choice. No matter your politics, every family wants a say in where their children go to school. Even those who fight against other families' right to choose schools, they consistently exercise "choice" for their own children. The good news is Americans are making choices in more and more aspects of their lives and the pressure to give families a say in what happens to their children will keep growing. If we truly believe in a free public education, children should not be automatically assigned to schools based on how much rent or mortgage their parents can afford. That's not free or equitable. That's a price tag.

Second, our society is in a relentless march towards more personalization, and this will eventually impact how we organize our schools. I often think of one of our five-year-old neighbors who was an expert in trains but "struggled" in school. He loved trains. He read everything he could get his hands on about them and had incredible content knowledge. Instead of listing all the ways he didn't "fit into" school, how could we create a school that "fit around" him. Our families just need permission to hope for something better for their children. Silicon Valley's biggest innovations are not technology solutions, they are the new business models facilitated by technology. So what will new school models look like going forward?

The shift towards choice and personalization will happen over a generation but there is no turning back at this point.

In your ThinkSchools blog, you highlight the benefits of personalized learning and design thinking as solutions to one-size-fits-all public education models. What's the relationship between the two and how can classrooms, schools, or systems take a first step to embrace that paradigm?

My interest in personalized learning kind of happened all at once. At work, I have the privilege of visiting a number of high-performing charter, district and private schools. These schools are doing incredible work, yet after great gains, their students seem to be hitting these stubborn "ceilings" around reading comprehension, writing, college persistence, etc.

At the same time, my twin boys began kindergarten at their local neighborhood school. I observed a four-to-five-year grade level spread in academic ability among the five-year-olds in their classes. Our boys attended a "'good" school, and the teachers did many of the things I'd want to see as an educator and a parent. But it became painfully obvious that many children were not getting what they needed academically, which also impacted them emotionally. One kindergartner wrote a letter to the teacher begging her to teach her some new math content while another five-year-old arrived at the conclusion that she was no good at math because everything seemed over her head.

I began to wonder if squeezing the proverbial lemon harder would get us the results we wanted or if we needed some radical new approaches.

I believe in personalized learning because I think we can do better than organizing school into boxes with thirty children and a teacher for thirty hours a week. I see school as more blank canvas than foregone conclusion.

Design thinking is simply an approach for educators to re-think school based on deep understanding of what students and families want/need. I'm on the board of 4pt0 Schools which uses design thinking to help education entrepreneurs launch Tiny Schools. With Tiny Schools, we are rapidly testing new school concepts with students and families participating at the beginning of the design process.

Now using student input may sound obvious, but if you've ever created a high school schedule, you know that the deep human needs of students are at the end of a very long list of other priorities.

Another example of deprioritizing students' needs is in textbook adoption. Committees of adults spend hours poring over textbooks even though there is little to no research showing that textbooks are effective learning tools. Plus, textbooks are insanely expensive. If the text selection process were based on how kids actually interacted and learned from textbooks, I suspect we'd see some very different decisions being made.

It's counterintuitive, but once you decide what your innovation is, have actual kids inform the design of your innovation. I was just at Summit Schools with Diane Tavenner, who explained that their personalized learning platform relies heavily on student input. At every turn, Summit solicits feedback from students as the ultimate end user. They built the student-facing dashboard first and then they built the teacher interface. When in doubt, you don't seek expert judgement, you ask the kid.

> **ALEX'S ONE GOOD QUESTION:** As a parent, I value personalization, socio-emotional development and self-directed learning a lot more than I did as an educator. What do those seemingly disparate perspectives mean about high quality education for all children?

ONE GOOD QUESTION WITH NICOLE YOUNG: CAN STUDENTS AND TEACHERS IMPACT ED POLICY? (USA)

In fourth grade, I had my first experience with student advocacy. One day, following a classroom test, I noticed that our teacher, Mrs. Oppenheimer, had broken protocol with our classroom expectations. From my desk, I could clearly read all of the names and assigned chores on our laminated octopus chore chart. The chores included things like clap the erasers, wash the chalkboard, collect supplies, distribute supplies, front of line leader, and back of line leader. Some of these chores had a higher status than others: everyone wanted to clap erasers because you got to go outside for a little fresh air. The chart system was designed for every student to experience all of the chores equally. But on this particular day, Mrs. Oppenheimer made a rogue decision and assigned a different student to go clap the erasers. I was appalled! In my best fourth grade cursive, I wrote her a letter describing this grave injustice and left it on her desk at the end of the school day.

To this day, I'm still learning what policy advocacy looks like in practice. When I met Nicole Young, she had recently transitioned from education policy work in the Obama Administration to leading a high school in New Orleans. Talking with Nicole demystified advocacy for me, and helped me see how advocacy lives in seemingly small actions like the letter to my teacher, all the way up to federal policy development.

In what ways do our investments in education reveal our beliefs about the next generation's role in the world?

Particularly for children of color and low-income students, we are not creating students who can invent a new system, but students who can perform well in the current system. And we know that the current system is flawed. We need to be creating youth who can create a new system and disrupt this one.

Beyond the structural school redesign needs, I actually question how we include students' voice in the creation of that new system. What would the outcome be if we considered student voices at the table to be essential to the conversation, not elective? What if we didn't know anything about how the policies were made, and we could just invent the systems that our kids need?

How does that level of engagement start? It starts with individual schools and campuses. We're thinking about it more on our campus, but we're not great at it yet. We have an advanced seminar this year and the students brainstormed what they want to do to complete their capstone assignment. Instructors took their ideas and synthesized them into eight great options that students could choose from. We have to think about how to make that type of student voice the norm, not an isolated decision.

Other questions that we're asking ourselves: How do we have student or alumni voice on our Board? How do we have students direct change? As our students are starting to organize, we wonder if their role is to create a glorified social club or to help us drive changes on campus. These strategies are not just for my eleventh and twelfth graders. Elementary students have voices that can influence their learning space. So many adults are thinking about hallway transitions and how to avoid twenty kindergarteners piled up on each other every time they leave the room. Could kindergartners think through that? I think so! And as a result, their investment in that solution could work. It starts at the school level and then upwards to state policy.

What keeps us from elevating student voice from being a "nice to have" to an essential element of education policy advocacy? Socialization. We were raised to believe that the younger you are, the less important your voice is. The same way that you have to break down biases in other realms, we have to put as much emphasis around the limitations of age. It's important to recognize the science that, yes, youth brains are not developed in the same way as adults, but different doesn't mean deficient.

Are we talking about youth-led change or youth-informed change? In practice we start with youth-informed and then move towards youth-led. I don't know that we could get to a state or federal policy that was youth-led. But I think if you had a really progressive group of people, on a campus or in a district — you could get true youth leadership there. Start by giving students real problems to solve, asking for their ideas/needs, and then drafting a few models that might respond. Bring your drafts back to the youth council to test it with them.

What do education policy makers need to know about school leadership?

We've had backlash around sweeping federal education policies, but I think it's less about the content and more about the idea generation process. With No Child Left Behind (NCLB), teachers didn't feel that it was informed by real-life experiences in the classroom. I wonder if educators would have felt differently about NCLB if the process included youth and current teacher practitioners? Even a little bit of distance from teaching and school administration means that you've lost some memory of that experience.

Policy makers occasionally visit schools and feel like that glimpse is enough to inform their decisions. Everyone knows that when the Feds come to visit your classroom, it is going to be the best day. Even students know it! I would encourage policy makers to spend more time on listening tours and hosting idea generation sessions with teachers and administration.

Teachers and school leaders have to feel like their ideas can move from idea generation to real policy. Great ideas about what works on the ground may not translate directly to a policy. The gap is that policy makers think that, just because a teacher isn't talking about policy, they don't have anything to contribute. At the same time, teachers feel like since they don't speak the policy language, they are disempowered to offer their ideas.

It's almost like some parent-teacher dynamics. Yes! Parents know their children, but don't have the language around pedagogy to advocate for specific changes. If you ask parents what success looks like for their kids, they may say, "a happy, healthy life where they are secure." Many may place happiness at the center. When those same parents talk about other people's children, the success gets murkier. If we're focused on all children, then we should be able to back map their needs. Practitioners need more support to think about how to translate their ideas into education policy.

> **NICOLE'S ONE GOOD QUESTION:** What role does education play in realizing the parent's dream of success and happiness for every child?

ONE GOOD QUESTION WITH PETER HOWE: ARE WE INCENTIVIZING THE RIGHT BEHAVIORS FOR TEACHERS AND STUDENTS? (THE NETHERLANDS)

I first met Peter Howe during my visit to the United World College (UWC) campus in Maastricht, Netherlands, where he was Head of School. He had been on the faculty at the UWC campus in Trieste, Italy, and after our interview, he went on to lead the oldest campus in the network — UWC Atlantic in Wales.

I arrived at the campus early enough to watch young people congregating under the flags in the courtyard, hanging out on the benches in the open auditorium, teaching a zouglou dance class on the basketball court, and a bachata dance class in the cafeteria. During that visit with Peter, I was reminded of why I loved working with secondary students. Peter adeptly balances the big picture of education leadership, the realities of daily administrative needs, the politics of school networks, and always centers young people and their developmental needs.

In what ways do our investments in education reveal our beliefs about the next generation's role in the world?

I trained as an economist (then an art historian, then an educator), so I'm fascinated by this question. In Dan Ariely's *Predictably Irrational*, he gives us the bad news first: economics is built upon the entirely false premise that people are rational. The good news is that people are irrational in a predictable way. His experiments demonstrate how financial incentives to "do good" actually backfire.

The implication is that as soon as you provide monetary reward for "doing good," the action becomes transactional. People's sense of being valued is entirely different. When we think that we're acting on behalf of shared humanity, we do more. When we anticipate compensation for the same behavior, we calculate our value and actually refuse to perform for lower compensation.

Earlier this fall, Paul Tough's article in The Atlantic[43] pointed out the distinction between teachers who raise test results and those who raise character attributes. The teachers didn't overlap much across groups, they were either in one camp or the other. What he found was that the teachers who raised test scores were the ones being rewarded by their schools, but that the skills students really need for college readiness are the social-emotional ones. That's a great example of how our investments obscure what we project as the best outcome, in this case college persistence.

When we apply Ariely's premise to schools, the incentive should be placed on building community. If we build the real community expectation, all of our members are more likely to contribute to each other's success. When we apply financial incentives for some members, for example compensating teachers for student test results, the teachers narrow their focus and support, and as a result fewer students achieve at high levels. It's literally a waste of money and creates the wrong incentives at the classroom level.

My favorite professor used Hegelian dialectics to teach a course in behavioral accounting. He would post on the door how well we were doing in recounting, connecting, synthesizing, and using connections to build something new — at which point you were at the pinnacle of learning. Even though our content was economics, he rewarded our thought process over discrete test scores. To go back to our example, make sure that the finances are rewarding the behavior that you want. Then you don't waste money with incentive programs that go fundamentally against people's needs. People want to feel valued, and our investments should reflect that.

If schools could only accomplish one outcome for all students, and could guarantee that outcome for all students, what would it be?

Every kid has to have that sense of safety and security — however we define that. Research shows that the traumatized or stressed brain is not a thinking

---

[43] Tough, Paul "How Kids Learn Resilience" The Atlantic. June 2016 Issue.

brain. Kids in poverty have higher indicators on the ACE[44] scale of trauma and also higher suspension rates. Being a part of a community is the most important contribution to safety and security. Creating a sense of security isn't only about environmental stress but engendering intellectual safety as well. The classroom is not about individual student success, it's about collective success. No student pisses me off more than the top student who stops coming to class when it is close to the exam because they would rather study on their own. At that point, they're no longer modeling engagement, and their peers don't benefit from the tough or complex questions that could have been asked. How do we address needs on both ends of the spectrum? We should focus the first two months of the year on community building and not curriculum. Once you have the community established and students are in inquiry-based learning, the curricular work will move more quickly. All of the students will have that sense of safety, trust, and willingness to admit that they don't know something. That's when learning can really occur!

> **PETER'S ONE GOOD QUESTION:** Why are you here? I ask this to every student who comes to my office, which is usually in a disciplinary context. I think that you can extend the question to educational institutions, too — Why are you doing X? Why are you doing it that way?

---

[44] In a 1998 study, The Center for Disease Control and Kaiser-Permanante identified ten potential adverse childhood experiences that may contribute to trauma and health outcomes in adults: physical, emotional, or sexual abuse, physical or emotional neglect, adults experiencing incarceration, mental illness, substance abuse, divorce, and mothers being treated violently. Subsequent ACES scales include community and environmental factors like racism, bullying, and community violence.

WHAT ARE YOU WONDERING?

SUSAN WONDERS: Will we be investing in the capabilities of thinking critically and creatively, and problem solving with the deep cultural responsiveness we will need to navigate an increasingly changing world?

ALEX WONDERS: As a parent, I value personalization, socio-emotional development and self-directed learning a lot more than I did as an educator. What do those seemingly disparate perspectives mean about high quality education for all children?

NICOLE WONDERS: What role does education play in realizing the parent's dream of success and happiness for every child?

PETER WONDERS: Why are you here? I ask this to every student who comes to my office, which is usually in a disciplinary context. I think that you can extend the question to education institutions too – Why are you doing X? Why are you doing it in that way?

When you think about voice and power in education decisions, who do you picture? What did you already know about education decision-making that was challenged by these interviews?

As you reflect on your one good question —

- Think about your audience: Which voices were missing from this chapter? Who are the experts for your wondering?
- Think about your context: What opportunities do the youngest learners have to influence their own education? What types of decisions do you trust youth to make for themselves?
- Think about your timing: Are you trying to get clarity on what has occurred or on what could be?

WHICH ADULTS SHOULD HAVE AGENCY IN SCHOOL DECISIONS?

CHAPTER 8

WHEN TONY MONFILETTO[45] and I first spoke in 2015, the United States was in the early years of adopting the Common Core State Standards (CCSS). Each state was deciding how they would adopt these standards, how they would assess student progress towards them, and how they would support teachers in delivering new curricular expectations. During a call in 2021, Tony shared his latest wonderings with me, and he's still questioning who should have agency in school design, but this time, he is focused on a broader audience.

Tony is championing a move away from accountability towards reciprocity. When he traces the origins of The Reciprocity Project, it dates back to the waning success of Common Core State Standards. By 2019, ten years after the earliest introductions of the standards, twenty states which had previously adopted CCSS had "repealed, revised, or rolled back parts of the program."[46] Tony saw this as an opportunity to consider what would replace the Standards. He was part of a collective of educators and community organizers who started

---

[45] See Chapter 4: One Good Question with Tony Monfiletto: Are the right people in the school redesign process?

[46] Goldstein, Dana. "After 10 Years of Hopes and Setbacks, What Happened to the Common Core?" The New York Times, December 6, 2019. https://www.nytimes.com/2019/12/06/us/common-core.html. Accessed May 10, 2021.

thinking about the purpose of school. They brought their wondering to a variety of communities around the country to hear from elders and young people in Tony's native New Mexico, as well as in Memphis, Minneapolis, Rhode Island and Hawai'i.

Before starting the national conversation, Tony offered this hypothesis, "A school is the missed community asset. Not only are current schools separate from the community, sometimes they are alienating, making communities poorer and less healthy." The intersection of the decline of the Standards movement and the COVID-19 health pandemic actually inspired a new possibility for the role of schools. Instead of measuring schools by reading scores and graduation rates, what if we measured schools by the ways they contributed to the health and wealth of their communities?

> "We began by asking key questions that it seemed no one was asking: 'What can we learn from community health workers about the impact of social determinants and root causes of inequity?'; 'Why does race play out as the most important social determinant of education?'; 'Why are we content with a few winners and many losers in our school outcomes?'; and 'What if the goal of school was to make communities healthier and more prosperous?'"
>
> - The Reciprocity Project[47]

During a conversation with Black community members in Memphis, they talked about how schools could have an impact on a healthier community. When pushed to think about metrics, a participant offered preventative care as a metric for a wellness-focused school. For example, if this school is effective, more community residents will receive preventative health care. More preventative health care in Black communities could lead to early detection of chronic and life-threatening illnesses, and maybe even longer life expectancy rates. School would then be seen as an asset to how that community operates by actively contributing to positive outcomes for the local population. This is what a reciprocal relationship between schools and communities could produce. Ultimately, the local community members would name the outcomes that matter most for their well-being and prosperity. Together, they would then

---

[47] *The Reciprocity Project.* https://thereciprocityprojecttrp.org/ 2020. Accessed March 18, 2021.

identify the metrics that demonstrate how well the school is contributing to their community outcomes.

The Reciprocity Project doesn't claim that all of their redesigned schools will center the same needs or metrics, but that every school will be responsive to their specific community's vision. Which stakeholders does Tony think are the right people to lead this school redesign? Not traditional educators. He fears that the education community doesn't have the best track record for building deep, trusting, reciprocal community relationships. Tony is counting on increased agency among community organizers and public health leaders to develop this new school model.

In this chapter we hear from leaders who, like Tony Monfiletto, wonder which adults should have agency in school decisions. Kaya Henderson (USA), Peter Howe (Canada/The Netherlands), and Ellen Moir (USA) explore agency for teachers — what roles can they have in advancing transformative instruction? Dr. Denese Shervington (USA) and Fabrice Jaumont (USA) explore agency for parents in selecting schools and organizing around their family's needs. Allan Golston shares observations about traditional school districts where students and educators drive the learning.

ONE GOOD QUESTION WITH KAYA HENDERSON: WHAT WILL MAKE MY HEART SING? (USA)

When Kaya Henderson left her high-profile role as the chancellor of the District of Columbia Public Schools (DCPS), I was really curious about what she would do next. I jumped at the chance to interview her so I could learn more about how she was approaching her transition and professional decisions. I've always thought that it's hard to build your vision for an entrepreneurial endeavor when you're working full time to deliver on someone else's goals. I wanted to know how Kaya was making space to develop the next phase of her career.

In what ways do our investments in education reveal our beliefs about the next generation's role in the world?

The US has invested in two things in public education that are fundamentally wrong. The first one? Perpetuating really low expectations for kids. When you look at our education investments over the last twenty to thirty years, the focus has been low-level proficiency in a handful of subject areas. That indicates a fairly low expectation about what kids can accomplish. It reveals our belief that if schools can just get the moderate level of proficiency, then they will have done their job. We seem to believe that low to moderate proficiency is the goal for some kids. For wealthy kids, we believe they also need international trips, art and music, foreign language, and service experiences. Those investments, made both by wealthy families and wealthier schools, point to greater expectations for those students.

I had the very good fortune to grow up in a family that started out poor but transcended to the middle class over the course of my childhood. I was blessed to have a mother who had us traveling the world, ensured that I spoke a foreign language, took horseback riding, and participated in Girl Scouts. But

I had cousins who came from the exact same place as I did, whose parents and schools didn't share those expectations. Some of them attended the magnet elementary with me, so even when their parents didn't have high expectations, good public schools put us on the same trajectory.

When I became chancellor of District of Columbia Public Schools (DCPS), my expectations were based on my personal experiences. I believe that schools have to inspire kids to greatness. What I saw, however, were people trying to remediate kids to death. So I inherited a district where people weren't teaching social studies and science, and where arts and foreign language programs were paid for by some PTAs because some parents recognized the needs even when the district didn't recognize them. What I saw were different expectations for different kids, and the investments followed suit. Our goal was to recreate these rich experiences, both enrichment and academic, for all kids.

The second investment that cripples US education? Systems that are built for teachers we don't believe in. We try to teacher-proof the things that we want teachers to do. But what if we give teachers what is worthy of them, piques their intellectual curiosity, makes them want to learn, push and challenge them; then teachers would rise to expectations in the same way that kids do.

One of the things that we did in DCPS was to significantly raise teachers' salaries and radically raise expectations. Lots of people were not happy about it, but the people who were happiest? Our best teachers! They were already rising to the highest expectations and saw the salary increase as validation for their work.

We reinvented our curriculum with the idea that every single course should have lessons that blow kids' minds. We designed what we called Cornerstone Lessons — the lesson that kids will remember when they are grownups. For example, when we're teaching volume in math, it coincides with a social studies unit on developing nations of the world. So, students can learn to design a recyclable water bottle in a few different dimensions to help developing countries get better access to water. They then build the prototypes for the containers and test them out. Lessons like that make you remember volume in a different way.

We wanted one Cornerstone Lesson in each unit for a total of five over the year. We designed lessons for every grade level, every subject area. When we designed the Cornerstone lessons, we mandated that teachers teach that lesson. What happened? Everyone used them and demanded more! Teachers wanted to have three or four Cornerstone Lessons for each of their units.

How do we get parents to opt into public schools at scale?

I had families tell me that I needed to do a better marketing job, that I wasn't selling DCPS enough. They compared us to charter schools with glossy brochures. When I started, the product that we had to market wasn't good enough. I didn't want to duplicate the negative experiences parents were getting: great marketing but then a disappointing product.

The first year that I was chancellor at DCPS, we didn't lose any kids to charters. That was monumental! After forty consecutive years of enrollment decline, we had five consecutive years of enrollment growth. We laid a foundation with a good program, then we listened to parents. We combined what they wanted, with what we knew kids needed, and rebuilt the system from the ground up. Our competitive advantage is that we are not boutique schools. We are like Target: we have to serve lots of different people and give them different things. As a district, our challenge is to guarantee the same quality of product, regardless of location. What are we going to guarantee to every family and how will every family know that?

We started by re-engineering our elementary schools. Some schools had been operating for so long without social studies, that they didn't know how to schedule for it. It meant creating sample schedules for them and hiring specialist teachers. Once we could tell parents that every school would have XYZ programs, they didn't have to shop for it anymore! Then we moved on to middle school and guaranteed advanced and enrichment offerings at every campus. Then we did the same at the high school level and significantly expanded AP courses. Today, all of our high schools offer on an average thirteen AP courses. Even if there are kids who have to take the AP course twice to pass the test, they do it. We know that the exposure to that level of academic rigor prepares students for college.

DCPS was a district where families came for elementary, opted out at middle school, and then maybe came back for a handful of high schools. So we looked at the boutique competitor schools and added a few of those models to DCPS too.

You do have to sell your schools, but there's no better advertisement than parents saying, "I love this school!" Some of our schools that were never in the lottery now have a ton of applicants! We were careful not to build things on charismatic people, but to build systems so that these gains would be sustainable. Now parents that never would have considered DCPS are clamoring for our schools.

Kids are kids, no matter where in the country they live. The cost of education is static. If we are serious about this education, we have to make some different decisions and put the money behind it. We've seen ten consecutive years of financial surplus in DC, at a time when the country was falling apart. I was even more lucky that three different mayors prioritized education and put the money in the budget. You can't expect schools to do more for the same dollars. You have to invest in innovation funds.

KAYA'S ONE GOOD QUESTION: Literally, my question is what is the best use of my time moving forward? When you're running a district, you are in the weeds. You don't know about all of the new and exciting things in the space. Right now, I'm being deliberate about exploring the sector and that's important. I want to figure out what will make my heart sing!

Right now, I'm obsessed with the intersectionality between housing, education, jobs, and healthcare. This old trope that if we just "fix" education, is garbage. I'm not saying it's linear or causal, but it's necessary to work on more than one issue affecting families at a time, and the efforts have to be coordinated and triangulated. Some of the most exciting things on the horizon are people like Derwin Sisnett, who is working to re-engineer communities for housing to be anchored around high performing schools and the community is replete with healthcare services and job training that the community needs to improve.

ONE GOOD QUESTION WITH DR. DENESE SHERVINGTON: HOW DO WE RE-ENGAGE THE BLACK MIDDLE CLASS IN PUBLIC EDUCATION? (USA)

When I moved home to New Orleans in 2016, there was a billboard campaign called #sadnotbad that shared public health data about the levels of post-traumatic stress disorder and depression in post-Katrina youth in the city. The campaign caught my attention because I had just completed a project to open a new, private high school exclusively for youth with multifaceted special needs and underlying psychosocial support. For months, I was deeply immersed in progressive special education models to increase agency for young people with learning differences. I kept imagining how different it might feel for a young person who had been labeled with an emotional disorder or behavioral disorder to actually understand their experience as depression or a response to trauma.

Dr. Denese Shervington is a psychiatrist and expert in trauma-informed practices who leads the agency behind the #sadnotbad campaign. Institute for Women and Ethnic Studies is a public health institute in New Orleans that combines advocacy, health education, research and direct services to improve wellness across the community. Like with so many of these interviews, what began as a conversation about my question quickly gave way to a completely unrelated wondering.

In what ways do our investments in education reveal our beliefs about the next generation's role in the world?

I think the investment is in trying to find a formula that can get more children in line so that they won't be a nuisance anymore. We're not creating learners and thinkers. We're creating an underclass of Black children who can step in line and can continue to serve the service industry in New Orleans. It's really hard as a middle-class Black person here because you have to question your own stuff. Enough of us in the Black middle class have gotten out of public education, and now we're oppressing those youth and families who still rely on public education. When I go into the schools and see the kids, I hurt.

I'm too old to not speak the truth.

- Dr. Denese Shervington

Schools here now are such a disappointment. My kids went to public schools in New Orleans. At that time, in the 1980s, 1990s, early 2000s, if you were poor but you had encouragement around education in the home or your community, you could still go to the public schools and be okay. You can't do that anymore. Our schools are actually traumatizing the children. I was in an elementary school two weeks ago observing kindergarteners and first graders. They were nervous. I can't imagine how you learn when you are so nervous. A few kids, based on their personality, those who do well under pressure, will do well, but that's not most children. They had to stand in line and do these rote things like "tracking the teachers with your eyes." The schools do these standard things that they think creates discipline, but it's not personalized. It feels like you're in a military school, or, at worse, in a prison.

The Black middle class — we have abandoned our children. I don't know any Black middle-class parents who are sending their kids to these schools. They're sending their kids to private schools. That means we don't care about what's going on with those who are less able to advocate for themselves. I don't think that white middle class New Orleanians would tolerate that kind of treatment for their children either. It bothers me when we're talking about how great the charter schools are here when this basic level of humanity does not exist.

For me, I think the progress is going to have to start with us. This new integration has not served us, so how do we get back to a collective consciousness and feel responsible for all of our children? Mine have succeeded, yours will succeed. But until every child has the capacity, your children could be dragged down by others. These are all of our children.

Schools are beginning to implement trauma-informed care models to support students with chronic negative behaviors. Is this work best for individual cases or can entire school communities benefit from trauma-informed pedagogies?

There are two things that all schools need to consider when implementing mental health supports: overall school climate and accurate diagnoses of root causes.

If you want to deal with mental health, you can change 80% now by addressing the school climate. Don't feel sorry for poor Black kids. Love them and have really high expectations for them. I'm borrowing from Dr. Andre Perry who says that you don't have to punish our kids into learning. The No Excuses school models have a disrespect and disregard of our children's humanity. Start with changing those practices.

Eighty percent of our kids are being misdiagnosed in special education. Most progressive school communities provide behavioral health, but the root causes are not behavioral, they're emotional. The behaviors are the end products of things happening inside. These kids are traumatized. When a kid is displaying a lot of behavioral dysfunctions, it's usually because there's something happening that they don't have any control over, and they can't communicate it. They don't have the language sophistication to talk about their feelings, so they show you. Until a student is properly diagnosed, s/he won't get the proper treatment. This goes back to the first condition: you have to care about the student and love them as an individual to wonder why they're misbehaving.

Schools with strong student support teams will, at the very least, ask about motivations for student behaviors before they start a functional behavioral assessment. The majority of school-based practitioners have never heard of #SadNotBad. How do we get practitioners to understand this?

It's like we're trying to do "fast mental health." You really have to spend time building relationships for the children to trust you and feel safe. If you start with the attitude that Black children are not inherently bad, or inferior, then it makes you want to do some stuff differently. A high level of love and caring means that you don't stop at the first question. You are driven to ask why and keep asking why until you really get to the source. That heart is not unique to Black educators. At Jean Gordon School, my children had a white principal who deeply believed that all children deserve to be loved, cared for, and educated.

We also need to pay attention to our adolescents, male and female, who are gender nonconforming. We're doing a Twitter chat focused on LGBT teens for suicide prevention month. If the kid is in a school where there is at least one adult with whom they can connect, it makes a difference. We need a safe space for the kids to interrogate what's going on in their lives. One of our health educators tells the story of a kid, who was having a lot of challenges at school, asking, "Can people be gay? Can boys be gay? Can I be gay?" That could be a benefit of the Teach for America (TFA) corps. They are more likely to create safe space for kids to be different and may themselves be gender nonconforming. Most traditional and/or older Black educators still struggle with this.

Whenever I talk about trauma in schools in New Orleans, it's not just due to Katrina or community divides. For many of these kids it's about the intrafamilial violence that they're experiencing around identity. Every community can benefit from these practices.

DENESE'S ONE GOOD QUESTION: What do I contribute to the process of healing and becoming whole for us in the Black community?

ONE GOOD QUESTION WITH ELLEN MOIR: WHAT'S TRUST GOT TO DO WITH IT? (USA)

In 1997, I was completing my undergraduate degree in secondary education and French, and that spring I started applying for teaching jobs in the greater St. Louis area. I was deeply committed to disrupting traditional education practices, leading with my social justice lens. I wanted to change the trajectory for Black and Brown kids whose schools and educators underestimated their genius. I wanted to teach in communities like the one I grew up in and thought, "who else is going to work in our neighborhoods and really love our students?"

For my first year teaching high school French, I taught at McCluer High School in the Ferguson-Florissant School District. I had a cadre of amazing veteran teacher mentors in the building who helped me deepen my pedagogical practices and student-engagement practices. It took me years to realize how fortunate I had been to have a strong balance of trust and guidance from mentor teachers in my first year. When I met Ellen Moir, founder of The New Teacher Center, her work on strengthening support for beginning teachers resonated with me.

In what ways do our investments in education reveal our beliefs about the next generation's role in the world?

First, let us acknowledge the world that we thought our kids would inherit. We are finally getting out of the past, in which we designed our schools to train kids to grow up and work in factories. We are finally investing in preparing kids for the future (or, at least as far as we can envision it) — a future society and economy that requires meaningful connection, trusting relationships, and creativity to solve the increasingly complex problems we'll face.

228

In some ways, we're trying to hold tight to the reins of defining what the next generation's role will be. We're trying to define it by applying our current frameworks, e.g., what our current jobs, economy, relationships, and geopolitical context look like. In reality, though, we can't really define it for this generation. They'll define it themselves. They're already starting to do that by pushing our adult thinking on how people learn, how people form meaningful connections with each other, and what innovation and social change look like. Teachers are shifting their practice to meet the needs of this generation. What if we shifted what schools looked like to better meet those needs, too?

We're preparing kids to grapple with complex problems by investing in teachers who can build their critical thinking and empathy skills. Investing in those teachers means personalized, one-to-one, on-the-job support, etc. Essentially, we're teaching teachers now how to engage in trusting relationships and creative problem solving in their practice, so that they can authentically bring those experiences to life in the classroom.

You speak passionately about trust at the center of effective teacher feedback and that the complexity in improving teaching is not the "what" but more of the "why" and "how." How do you link trust with the "why" and "how" for more effective teaching?

Trust *is* an essential component of the how. Building trusting relationships between new teachers and their mentors (or helping new principals build trusting relationships with their teachers) is critical in order for any of our other work to happen.

We build trust by starting from a place of respect, assuming positive presuppositions, and remembering that we all share a common goal: to ensure that our students receive the best education possible. When we mentor new teachers, one of the first things we work with them on is creating a safe and positive learning environment. For teachers, building trust with their students is critical in creating a learning environment in which students respect one another and are willing to take risks in order to learn and grow.

Ultimately, our work is not about telling new teachers what to teach. It's about coaching each new teacher to find *their best way* to reach all students. And teacher development needs to be contextualized and tied to student learning outcomes.

In a trusting community of practice, we can provide rich feedback that supports helping each teacher move up the learning line.

> **ELLEN'S ONE GOOD QUESTION:** If the most critical student competencies for the future are about addressing complex problems with diverse populations, how can we better prepare teachers to do the same?

ONE GOOD QUESTION WITH FABRICE JAUMONT: HOW PARENT ORGANIZING LEADS TO REVOLUTION (USA)

In 2005, when I was still teaching in Queens, a group of families came to visit our secondary school. They asked to meet with a few teachers about their vision for a new dual-language French school within the New York City Department of Education (NYCDOE). I was the mom of a six-month old, and I was already raising her in French, our family's language. When these parents came to visit our school and seek our advice, I realized two things: bilingual families saw us as experts and families have the power to ask for the public-school education that they want for their children. These families were inspired by their own children and were committed to advocating as long as they needed for a public school option even if it meant their children might not get to attend the school. They found a passionate partner in Dr. Fabrice Jaumont, Education Attaché for the Embassy of France.

As a result of their advocacy, the first French dual-language program in a public school in New York opened in Brooklyn in 2007. By the time we had this conversation in 2015, Fabrice had supported ten parent organizing groups to successfully lobby the NYCDOE to open French dual-language programs for their neighborhood schools. Over the years, parent organizing groups from other heritage[48] or minoritized languages sought out Fabrice's counsel as they led advocacy efforts to open dual-language programs in Japanese, Italian, German, Russian, Arabic, and Korean.

In what ways do our investments in education reveal our beliefs about the next generation's role in the world?

Part of my research, and the recent book that I have published, *Unequal Partners: American Foundations and Higher Education Development in Africa*

---

[48] Heritage language refers to a familial language that isn't reinforced in public or formal settings.

(Palgrave-MacMillan), focuses on philanthropy and American foundations, particularly those that make financial investments in education development in Africa. I also work with philanthropists on a regular basis through my work in bilingual education in the United States. I raise funds for my programs which provide services to schools and support the needs of dual language students in various settings. Coming from France, which has a tradition of state-controlled support to education, I have always been intrigued by the U.S. philanthropic culture and tradition of "giving back to the community," which encourages people, wealthy or not, to contribute financially or by volunteering their time and expertise. This, I find, can have a tremendous impact on children, schools, and communities. I believe it creates better chances for the next generation and helps them access quality programs, equal opportunities, and the right conditions to grow and play an active role in society.

I find it inspiring to see people giving money willingly — on top of the taxes they pay — to improve a city's or the country's education system. The fact that these individuals want to make a difference through their actions and financial contributions is a social contract that I find worthy of our attention. If done well, with the buy-in of communities, it can have an impact on hundreds of thousands of children that would not necessarily have these chances — even within the context of a strong centralized system. This tradition of giving also sends a very strong and hopeful message, which is carried on from one generation to the next. As a child, you might have received support from the generosity of someone, perhaps even someone whom you never met. As an adult, you might want to be that generous donor and help a child experience the things that he or she couldn't have experienced otherwise.

We can criticize this tradition too. A lot has been said about the Gates Foundation's failure to improve education despite its best intentions, ambitious programs, and the billions of dollars that it poured into transforming schools and educational models. One could ask why, in the first place, foundations and wealthy individuals try to change school systems. Should we not tax these individuals more so that wealth could be redistributed through a more democratic process rather than an individual's pet projects? Surely, the future of our children should not depend on the largesse of the super rich.

Sometimes foundations are seen as having a corrosive impact on society. In my book, I analyze these critics' views of US foundations in Africa. I also provide a new understanding of educational philanthropy by using an institutional lens that helps me avoid the traps and bias that I pinpointed in the discourse of foundation opponents. In my opinion, grantors and grantees have an unequal relationship from the start. As a result, the development agenda is either imposed by the money holders, or "adjusted to please the donor" by money seekers who just want to secure the funds or win the grant competition. To reconcile this discrepancy, I propose that philanthropists and grant recipients place their relationship on an equal footing and engage in thorough conversations which start with the needs of and seeks input from all actors. This can generate more respect and mutual understanding, and strengthen each step of the grantmaking process, from building a jointly-agreed agenda to tackling the issues more efficiently.

Too often in public education, language immersion and international education are only offered to children from middle-class environments. The community of bilingual/dual-language schools in the New York City Department of Education make an effort to promote immersion for students from diverse backgrounds. What could that choice of intentional diversity mean for the future of the city?

In several contexts of education, immersion and international education is too often reserved for children of the affluent. The community of public bilingual schools that I have helped develop in New York and in other cities provides access to quality programs to children of diverse socioeconomic and ethnic backgrounds. Dual language programs have existed for about ten years in New York City and are gradually replacing traditional models of bilingual education programs which focus on teaching English to immigrants. This original model was created in the 1960s through the civil rights movement when immigrants asked that their children be taught in both English and their home language so that they were given equal chances to succeed in American society.

The new model of dual-language education focuses on bilingual education for all. At least that is how I see it. Children of all linguistic backgrounds spend half of their school time in English and the other half in a target language. They learn to write and read in both languages as well as study content such as math, science, and social studies through both languages. For the last ten years, I have helped linguistic communities create dual-language programs in French, Japanese, Italian, German, Russian, Arabic, and Korean. The families that I have met are motivated by a strong desire to maintain their linguistic heritage — more so than develop English, which children are acquiring naturally through their surroundings. For these families, schools should put more value on children's heritage language and culture, and help them make an asset of their bilingualism.

Also, I see an increasing number of American families — who only speak English at home — value the benefits of bilingualism, bi-literacy, and biculturalism. They, too, ask that schools help them grow multilingual competence in children, and encourage students to acquire new languages as early as possible, preferably through dual-language or foreign-language immersion. That's good news for any country whose citizens are willing to open their minds to the world and the world of others by mastering languages and discovering new cultures. In my view, this learning process has the potential to foster more respect, tolerance, and understanding of others. Ultimately, I believe this can foster more peace. Moreover, when parents demand that schools provide this kind of bilingual education, it becomes a true revolution. And this is the title of my next book: *The Bilingual Revolution.*

FABRICE'S ONE GOOD QUESTION: Whether we help improve a public school in Brooklyn or a university in Dar es Salaam: How can we make sure that all actors in the communities that we try to impact are consulted and given an equal voice in the conversation, so that the solutions we may bring are indeed conceived together and do correspond to real needs?

ONE GOOD QUESTION WITH ALLAN GOLSTON: INVESTING IN INSTRUCTION MATTERS MOST (USA)

When I heard Allan Golston speak about his high school experience in Denver, I knew that I wanted to interview him for this series. I had never met Allan before, but his recounting of the academic sorting that happened in his high school building made me think of my own earliest observations and questions about education equity and access. My grandmother was a secretary in Lafayette Parish Public Schools, and she guided all of my early school access — researching programs and opportunities that would broaden my exposure. As a result of her advocacy, I tested for and, in second grade, started to attend enrichment classes under our school district's gifted and talented program. Being accepted into this program as a Black girl who lived in a historically Black neighborhood with Black-led schools meant leaving my neighborhood school for a long bus ride to a new-to-me part of town. Apparently, there were not enough students in my neighborhood elementary school for the district to assign a gifted enrichment teacher to our campus. Ironically, our neighborhood middle school, Paul Breaux, was home to the first dedicated gifted enrichment program in the parish. I attended classes there through eighth grade and by age ten, I noticed how much more agency our enrichment program afforded us in comparison to my uncles, neighbors, and friends in the traditional classrooms. I wondered why we got these types of learning experiences and other students didn't.

Allan Golston is the president of the United States Program at the Bill and Melinda Gates Foundation. The US Program works to ensure everyone in the United States can learn, grow, and get ahead, regardless of race, gender, ethnicity, or family income. This includes a considerable focus on K-12 education, pathways, and post-secondary success. In this interview Allan explores how to eliminate this education caste system in the United States and how investments in locally relevant problem-solving might make the biggest difference.

In what ways do our investments in education reveal our beliefs about the next generation's role in the world?

I believe that our investments reveal that the next generation is obviously the future. Our future depends on how well we prepare our students, regardless of their background. Demographic population in this country is shifting in dramatic ways. The next generation will need to be socially mobile and solve the world problems of the future and do it with fundamental skill sets — think critically, solve problems, and apply knowledge in complex ways. One way that we believe this is possible is through high-quality education. High-quality education only happens if it's supported by great teachers. Fundamentally, this is why we invest in education: access to a high-quality education that prepares young people for their future-career or post-secondary studies and then career — we think that is mission critical.

The Gates Foundation's education strategies are prioritized and focus heavily on the investment in professional development. We would frame that in our work as feedback on teacher effectiveness. What's clear from our experiences and the research is that what happens between a teacher and student in the classroom is one of the most important investments that you can make that drives student outcomes. Once you say that, then that means that you have to focus on instruction. If you focus on instruction, how do you dramatically improve and sustain high-quality instruction so that it benefits all kids? That means feedback for teachers, and personalized professional development for teachers that helps them improve their practice. If you look at the foundations' investments, that is one of the critical paths and one of our top three education priorities.

You've spoken publicly about the education caste system that you experienced in your Denver high school. Do you think that it's possible to eliminate that in the US and if so, what change does that require?

I do think it's possible. Several reasons that I know it's possible, is that we see it working in certain places and that gives us a lot of confidence that we can do this. If you think about education as an equalizer, but then access to high-quality education isn't accessible to all, then education itself becomes a cause of inequity. Education for too many of our young people depends on ZIP codes and parent income levels. It's a huge problem and yet we know what it takes to solve it. If you look at where it's working across the country, students are thriving and achieving. The four things that we believe make it possible:

1. High expectations for all students
2. Great teaching that is sustainable for all teachers and all kids
3. More personalized education for all students
4. Having students and educators at the core, driving the learning

After a recent learning trip in eastern rural Kentucky, a resource-limited area further devastated by the decline of the coal industry, these principles were borne out in clear ways. What I was struck by most was seeing the fourth principle in action. Educators in this community were at the core of the work and they were unwavering in their responsibilities to students. I contrasted this with many visits to urban resource-limited areas, where often you hear educators say that they don't believe all kids can learn. They list a litany of realities (poverty, hunger, parent absenteeism) that almost fall in the conversation as excuses. Yet in eastern Kentucky, down to the individual stakeholder, everyone refused to accept those same conditions as excuses and demonstrated the "whatever it takes" attitude. These educators were data-driven, believed in iterating with students, were deeply involved in student growth, and valued incremental growth and support. These are things that I think are extraordinary — they know the students' social struggles and still ensure that the families have access to food and can get basic needs met and get back on their feet, all without lowering expectations for student achievement.

I think that in rural areas, there is a sense of community that you don't see in urban settings. It's [more] natural based on the small size of their communities — everyone knows each other. The geographic dimensions create community urgency and agency that can be very difficult to duplicate in an urban setting. I also think that when you are in a resource-constrained environment, often you have to figure out how to get things done when you know that there are no additional resources coming. In rural areas, there is no hope of resources dramatically increasing — there won't be a better contract or more taxes — so, in those areas, educators have to think differently. Their mindset for how to get things done more quickly takes on a different dimension.

We tend to think of urban as a monolith as opposed to the sum of the parts. I've seen in some urban areas that, when they break down their geographic footprint into smaller footprints, they can duplicate the culture of community that exists more organically in rural settings — where educators know all the students. I believe it's possible.

> **ALLAN'S ONE GOOD QUESTION:** Why haven't we solved high-quality education for all children? That's what this country has to wrestle with.

WHAT ARE YOU WONDERING?

KAYA WONDERS: Literally, my question is what is the best use of my time moving forward? When you're running a district, you are in the weeds. You don't know about all of the new and exciting things in the space. Right now, I'm being deliberate about exploring the sector and that's important. I want to figure out what will make my heart sing!

DENESE WONDERS: What do I contribute to the process of healing and becoming whole for us in the Black community?

ELLEN WONDERS: If the most critical student competencies for the future are about addressing complex problems with diverse populations, how can we better prepare teachers to do the same?

FABRICE WONDERS: Whether we help improve a public school in Brooklyn or a university in Dar es Salaam: How can we make sure that all actors in the communities that we try to impact are consulted and given an equal voice in the conversation, so that the solutions we may bring are indeed conceived together and do correspond to real needs?

ALLAN WONDERS: Why haven't we solved high-quality education for all children? That's what this country has to wrestle with.

When you think about voice and power in education decisions, who do you picture? What did you already know about education decision-making that was challenged by these interviews?

As you reflect on your one good question —

- Think about your audience: Which voices were missing from this chapter? Who are the experts for your wondering?
- Think about your context: Whose voice has been historically barred from education decision-making in your community? What types of decisions do you trust parents to make for their children?
- Think about your timing: Are you trying to get clarity on what has occurred or on what could be?

WILL SCHOOL EVER BE ENOUGH TO IMPROVE SOMEONE'S TRAJECTORY?

CHAPTER 9

KNOW THAT THIS BOOK is all about asking your "one good question," a question that doesn't have an apparent answer and forces you to grapple with new perspectives. Until 2014, I was an education zealot. I really believed that if we solved societal needs in school, that we could impact other oppressive systems. That all changed when, on Saturday, August 9, 2014, Michael Brown Jr. was killed by Darren Wilson, a police officer in Ferguson, Missouri. At that time, I was leading a network of schools in St. Louis. One of our campuses, where my children attended school and where my offices were located, was directly across the street from the new St. Louis Metropolitan Police Headquarters. Our community was overcome with grief, anger, and uncertainty in the months that followed. As a Black mother, I was overwhelmed with the thought that I could not keep my own son safe. As a school leader who served majority Black and Brown students, I became consumed with the realization that our schools could not keep our students safe from police violence. At the time that I'm writing this chapter, I've just learned that one of our former elementary school students was killed at age 15, while riding his bike in a St. Louis neighborhood. My heart hurts for his family, friends, and our school community.

So while I am asking the question, "will school ever be enough to improve someone's trajectory?" *I know* that school alone will never be enough to change centuries of violence against Black and Brown bodies. It is difficult for me to remain neutral about the role of school. Am I intensely curious about how school could intersect with other sectors? Absolutely. Am I also clear that the institution of schooling was never designed to improve everyone's path in life? Absolutely. Some of you may struggle with this context. You may be thinking about the positive impacts that school had in your own family's trajectory. You may recall stories that I've told about my family's access to higher education and wonder, "Rhonda, aren't these stories proof that education can make the difference in someone's life?" I hear you. Stories of individual exceptionalism are always inspiring. But remember, I started asking "one good question" because I didn't have the answers. This book is a study in the power of questioning.

> What solutions are we potentially leaving unexplored if we assume that school alone can improve someone's trajectory? Which communities and populations are we ignoring if we think the only answer is to provide them more education in a system that wasn't actually designed for their success?

Before you read these final interviews, let's do an exercise. Think about where you are from or where you are currently living. In each of our communities, there is a well-documented timeline for who first had access to formal education institutions (always boys and men) and when every other marginalized group gained access to formal education (girls and women, enslaved and servant classes, immigrants/refugees/outsiders, people with disabilities, multilinguals, etc.). Were your early schools created by your public government? Were your early schools created by houses of worship and administered by religious leaders? Who was allowed to teach then? Who are your teachers today? What was in the early curriculum? The answers to these questions can help you identify who was the intended beneficiary of formal education in your community.

This is the final chapter and we've explored everything from language of instruction to education finance and youth development. In this chapter, we hear from leaders who all advocate for a collaboration between formal education AND at least one other sector. These leaders see school as a key component to changing the learner's life as well as society, but are clear that school cannot be the sole answer. Anu Passi-Rauste (Finland) explores the relationship between school and professional internships. Ana Ponce (USA) wonders about school and wraparound services for students and families. Derwin Sisnett (USA) looks at the intersection of new school development and new housing development, and Susan Baraghwanath (New Zealand) reflects on the role of school and parenting.

ONE GOOD QUESTION WITH ANU PASSI-RAUSTE: EDUCATION TO BUILD TALENT PIPELINES (FINLAND)

Have you ever had an internship? A pre-service rotation? A residency? A practicum? For some career paths, like teaching, it's common or required to have supervised practice before you can be certified to work independently. As an entrepreneur, I'm a passionate believer in providing paid internship and fellowship opportunities for young people. We work with high school students, opportunity youth, recent high school graduates, undergraduate students, and graduate students and design a series of learning and capstone projects for them on different teams in our nonprofit. For many of them, our internship is their first opportunity to work outside of retail, fast food, babysitting, or amusement parks. I think the best outcome is when our internship reinforces what they're learning in school or awakens a new professional interest. Until this conversation with Anu Passi-Rauste, I didn't realize how rare it is for workers in different sectors to get real-world experience before starting a career. Anu Passi-Rauste is a Finnish entrepreneur who, at the time of our interview, was dedicating her wondering to questions about innovative approaches to workforce development in the US and Finland.

In what ways do our investments in education reveal our beliefs about the next generation's role in the world?

I'm really encouraged that we're starting to see our education investments shift to include different projects and initiatives in which students are part of a bigger ecosystem and instrumental in designing our future. The new generation needs to be a part of collaboratively solving world problems. We don't know what the jobs will be in the future because the world is changing so rapidly. I want to see the future as a sustainable world, where people are empowered to grow and learn for their own success.

We see those expectations in the UN Sustainable Development Goals and on the national level in Finland. To transform our education system is a long process. Fifteen years ago, when I was a teacher, I experienced that the most fascinating way to teach was to learn together with the students. What I saw then was that when students had problems that they were interested in, they were self-motivated to dig deeper. As an entrepreneur, I have learned that the best part of my work is that I need to learn every day. We are social learners. The best part of being an entrepreneur is that we need to test all the time and validate our process. The scientific method is part of my daily life and part of my adult learning process. Education practice is slowly starting to incorporate this method into general pedagogy. The real positive inspiration is that you get interested by yourself and you start to follow some fields or topics and then identify what value you can bring there.

Although we focus on skills and competence-based education, those competencies aren't the only means to developing students for the future. Schools are still silos — they are physically isolated from society and within the buildings, school lessons are still divided into one-hour topics with related projects. We're still learning for the test and valuing extrinsic motivation over intrinsic motivation. My entrepreneurial career is focused on how the school is part of the big community and creating opportunities for schools and students to work together with companies, organizations, and civic groups. Organizations can learn from the students and give students meaningful problems to solve. It also gives forerunner companies the possibility to enhance their learning about next-generation employees and consumers. As a result, students get relevant learning beyond classes, more experience, and opportunities to find their own passion and motivation for learning.

Your past projects have centered on student agency in innovation and problem-solving. What does it mean for the greater society to have today's youth be an integral part of entrepreneurial solutions?

Today's learning is organized around problem-based learning, challenges and case studies. What if this could be done in close collaboration with our actual economic ecosystem? If we can bridge this gap, it helps us to employ the young graduates and build their courage, self-confidence, and attitude for lifelong learning and self-trust. We can create opportunities for students to feel integrated and valuable in greater society. We help students with their ideas and have industry experts who are willing to listen and coach them. In the end, students come up with brilliant solutions to company-based challenges or their own ideas for start-ups. This model also increases democratic opportunities for the broader population.

One thing that I've learned is that when students are really working on their own ideas, they want to be responsible for their own learning. It doesn't mean that they don't need support, but that they can then identify the support that they need. That's what creates a critical role for teachers, facilitators, and companies to respond to the students' needs. Access to community-supported learning needs to be a right for everybody. We still have work to do to refine the models that connect the employers and students. Under our new venture, LearnBrand, we want to give students an opportunity to apply the knowledge that they've learned, which is a critical part of the learning process. We focus on actionable learning where we engage people during their college and university studies. We give them real-world assignments and experience. We build a bridge between learners and employers and help both sides equally; students grow their practical skills and employers manage their future talent pipeline.

> **ANU'S ONE GOOD QUESTION:** How do we empower our students to keep their curiosity and growth mindset throughout their lives?

ONE GOOD QUESTION WITH ANA PONCE: IS SCHOOL ENOUGH FOR OUR KIDS? (USA)

When I interviewed Ana Ponce, she had been CEO of the Camino Nuevo Charter Academy school network in Los Angeles for fourteen years. The first time I visited one of their campuses, I sat in on a middle school advisory conversation. I had worked with middle school aged youth for twenty years at that point, but during this advisory, young people were being more vulnerable, supportive, and engaged with each other than I ever knew was possible. They had created a community with mutual accountability — one that lifted up their successes, called out their struggles, and kept the students most at risk for being pushed to the margins, centered in love. Ana Ponce had grown up a generation before with her Mexican immigrant family in the same high-poverty neighborhoods with the same border-crossing experiences as many of her students. In this interview, she shares how understanding the full lives of families impacts the way that Camino Nuevo sees and supports students in need.

In what ways do our investments in education reveal our beliefs about the next generation's role in the world?

Our mission at Camino Nuevo is to prepare students to succeed in life; we want our kids to be compassionate leaders, critical thinkers, and problem solvers and to thrive in a culturally connected and changing world. But we can't do this work alone. We need families to be our partners. That's why, from the beginning, when we opened our first school, one of our priorities was institutionalizing an authentic parent engagement program with a robust menu of support services. We try to get to know families and understand their needs. When a family needs help, our staff connects them with existing support services in our community. Our commitment to families is paying off: Nearly 100 percent of our students graduate and are college bound.

There is a perception that running an effective parent engagement and support services program costs millions of dollars. However, it's all about the partnerships and how schools integrate the support structures into the day. For example, our schools are able to offer mental health counseling because we partner with a nonprofit mental health provider in the community. We also partner with graduate schools that provide us with interns. Through this partnership model, we can provide services to about 2,000 youth at a fraction of the total cost. We have similar partnerships for our students to have access to the arts, science, mentoring, and afterschool programming. These resources and services are available in many communities.

Without dedicated funding available, so many schools feel like they have to choose between academic support and mental health support. Why not just rely on community agencies to respond to these needs?

Schools don't have to provide every direct service. However, it is time that schools embrace collaboration and coordination. As educators, we know when families are struggling because a family member will turn to a teacher, or staff member, they trust to ask for help. Sometimes we find out [about a need] because a student is acting out due to the stress or trauma imposed by a family's situation. That's when we can connect those families with support agencies. For example, when a child's family member has been deported, our staff has connected the student and their family to support services because we know how traumatic this situation can be for everyone. We do the same when we hear of a family who may be at risk of being evicted from their home. Everyone — from school leaders to custodians to office assistants – is trained on the referral process as well as our partnership philosophy. So if a school's office manager hears about a family in need, that person knows something can be done about it and knows who can connect the family to the services they need.

When we grow up in under-served communities and teach/lead in those same communities, we want to provide our students more access than we had. Is that enough? Does today's generation of (insert your demographic here) need something different than we did?

It gives me pause when I hear people say, "Is that enough?" What is enough? What does that mean? Ten years ago, I was meeting with a program officer who asked when our work would be "done" in the MacArthur Park community. [laughter]

What's happening here, in terms of the consequences of poverty, is so beyond what we can do as a school. When I think about what is enough, I know that school is not enough. We have a lot more to do and we need a lot more of us to do it. I believe that we need to create culturally reflective environments where our children are seeing themselves, and who they can become, on a daily basis. As people of color, we come into the education space and some stay for a few years, others stay longer. I don't think we are doing enough in diversifying the education workforce. I believe we need to do more to prepare people of color for college success so that we can recruit more teachers of color, more leaders of color in education and education adjacent fields.

It's important that our communities support more of us coming back in some way. It doesn't mean that you have to come back and live in the same community. You can "come back" in different ways — teach or lead in a school site, work in an education nonprofit. Our kids need to see us come back and inspire them. When they see people who look like them in positions of influence (principals, C-suite level organizational leaders, key board members) and engaging in different activities (in college fairs, arts programs, ethnic studies classes), their perception of what is possible for them begins to change.

Camino Nuevo students are getting a lot more, in many ways, than I or my peers did back in the day. For kids like me, high school completion was the exception, not the norm. And now I wonder if high school completion is enough for today's little Anas? In some ways it is. Our students get more personalized attention, more wraparound services, more enrichment opportunities, and more access to higher education than we had growing up in these neighborhoods. However, our kids still need more because the system is so broken and set up against their success. Our students need more than a solid educational foundation to make them competitive and to help them navigate the system. Higher education needs to rethink how it supports first-generation college students to [degree] completion. We have a solid track record of getting our kids to pursue higher education options and many of them are encountering significant barriers that most often are not academically related. What we are doing at Camino Nuevo is great and it is a lot "more," but I don't believe that it is enough because of the barriers our kids continue to face every day due to systemic injustice.

As a nation, we're struggling with low college completion rates. We're seeing a slight increase in graduation rates for Latinos, but a lot of our kids start college and don't finish. Education leaders and opinion influencers are rethinking the goals of K-12. I'm really concerned that more folks are thinking about creating alternate pathways for Latinos that don't include a college education. That's constantly on my mind. I know that my students, my kids, will need a college degree to be competitive and to be on the path to leadership and influential positions. I am committed to educating all our kids to be leaders in their communities and in their fields. When we start creating watered-down pathways to a job, we're not setting our students up to be leaders. What does that say about what we're really trying to do? Jumping to alternative pathways is a quick solution. But let's think about the consequences and examine what we as educators and what our institutions are not getting right. Let's not blame the kids just yet. Let's turn the mirror on ourselves.

> **ANA'S ONE GOOD QUESTION:** How do we move "average students" to attain higher levels of success beyond being at top of their class?

ONE GOOD QUESTION WITH DERWIN SISNETT: WHICH DO YOU BUILD FIRST, SCHOOLS OR COMMUNITIES? (USA)

I have visited hundreds of schools across the globe and I am usually focused on the people components — student experience, pedagogy, family and community engagement, and governance. A school is not the building — I've observed schools with the highest levels of student engagement and graduation rates that operated in portable classroom buildings. Every now and then, the school facilities are designed with pedagogy, instructional models, or values at the center. Site visits to those campuses inspire me in a different way to think about the investment in space as an investment in student engagement.

This interview with Derwin Sisnettt added another layer of education investment to consider: investment in space as an investment in the broader community. Derwin had leveraged his expertise in community development to design and creatively finance a public school campus that included a performing arts center and affordable housing. In the fall of 2016, I jumped at the chance to tour the newest campus of Gestalt Community Schools, a charter management organization in Memphis that Derwin co-founded. In this interview, he explores the opportunity for schools, especially in historic Black neighborhoods, to revitalize and redefine success with the community.

In what ways do our investments in education reveal our beliefs about the next generation's role in the world?

To me, investment is all about bringing opportunities to others that were given to me when I was a kid, whether it was from my parents, community members, or business folks. What I think we should bring to the table is time and thoughtfulness around this work. My work is not just about education. It is about the whole community. In the education reform movement, we've somehow convinced ourselves that if we overdo the classroom work, we'll somehow address all the issues that we need to address because of kids' "perseverance" and "resilience." If we get that part right, the students will somehow make it out of their neighborhood. The problem is, they make it "out" and you've left another void in the community. Education investment has to be more about compassion and more about giving something that actually represents a sacrifice.

Building the infrastructure doesn't necessarily ensure that people will take advantage of the service, that requires a shift in mentality. What you've built in Memphis, a mixed-use development for schools, affordable housing, and performing arts center, was a massive statement about the positive value of school and a bigger community. If you build it will they come?

I don't believe that if you build it, they will come. I believe if you build them, they will come. As much as we wanted to build the Town Center as quickly as possible, it was in our best interest to actually build the capacity of the school, families, and community first. We almost had to realize this lesson over time because it took us years to raise the dollars. When we opened the campus in 2016, we literally just transferred a school from one building to the next. It was not a difficult transaction for our organization. We were not wondering if we were going to meet enrollment. We had also developed a broader facilities strategy where Power Center Elementary would move into the older campus. Therefore, if you build them, the people in your community, to a place where they see access to education as the first step to change, then they will protect and engender sustainable change for others.

There is some discourse that high-performing schools lead to gentrified communities. How does that fit in the community development model?

In Atlanta, I met with an African American developer, who understands African American community, and he gave the best analogy about mixed-income communities. He said, this is like Orbitz, you don't know how much that person sitting next to you paid, but they got a seat on the plane. Education access should operate in the same ways to increase access for all youth. I grew up in New York where everybody paid $1.25 to get on the train. That train is accessible to everyone and eventually even Mayor Bloomberg got on that train. From millionaires to folks for whom it's hard to get $1.25, they all understand the value of the train and it gives them access to everything. We are all in the same vehicle. That's where we need to be with education. High-quality schools represent an opportunity to eliminate gentrification. It actually can inspire diverse communities. People start to value what the school is itself and they recognize that this is not something for poor people or rich people, this is something for people.

This is a human issue. That's quite frankly my concern with education reform, we call it a civil rights movement, but we don't actually have a call for humanity to do this work. It's just simply "all kids need a great education" and we don't drill down to why. The reason why is because of humanity. When I think about gentrification, the reason that happens is because somehow, we believe that this "thing" is so good now, this person shouldn't have it (anymore). We convince ourselves that we somehow earned this public good. No one in New York feels like they "earned" the A train. That's just the vehicle to get from point A to point B, and that makes it a right.

> **DERWIN'S ONE GOOD QUESTION:** Why are we missing the mark on diagnosing the problem with education reform? Do we have the wrong people asking the questions?

ONE GOOD QUESTION WITH SUSAN BARAGWANATH: THE ONLY WAY TO BREAK THE CYCLE OF POVERTY (NEW ZEALAND)

Susan Baragwanath is one of New Zealand's foremost educators who in 1995 founded He Huarahi Tamariki, a school for teenage parents in Wellington. When we met in 2014, I was in my final year running the school network that I had founded. In the United States, I had a cadre of mentors — educators who had designed new school models a decade earlier and were very generous with their time and lessons learned. In many ways, my mentors and I had a similar trajectory. We had been passionate, young teachers who were inspired by an academic and pedagogical vision to do school better. Susan's pathway to developing a new school model was quite different from my own. There was something really grounding about spending time with a veteran school founder, especially one who had navigated completely different political waters to do what was right for young people.

Susan had already taught for twenty years before she designed He Huarahi Tamariki. She had been working in Europe and returned home to Wellington as an assistant principal in a secondary school. One day she stumbled upon a fourteen-year-old giving birth in the school bathroom. She assisted with the birth and soon thereafter started working on how to keep this young mother engaged in school and parenting. Her vision for He Huarahi Tamariki came from holding those dual outcomes — school completion and healthy parenting — as equally important.

In what ways do our investments in education reveal our beliefs about the next generation's role in the world?

I have never been into deep thinking on education, and I am not much of a philosopher. As a practitioner for 37 years, I saw immense change from rote learning to the touch of an iPad. Show me a young person who knows the times tables and can write a sentence in the imperfect tense? But does it matter when they can use a calculator and Google? As a teacher I have always felt it was my duty to challenge a student to believe that they could do anything they wanted. It was up to me to provide the mechanism so they could achieve to the best of their ability. But now, in the twenty-first century, what mechanism is it exactly?

There has been huge investment in technology in recent years. This has facilitated both teaching and learning in ways that we previously couldn't imagine. The change is so dramatic that the traditional teacher now struggles to keep up. We used to joke that we needed to be "a page ahead of the kids." Now the joke is on us. Older teachers, with all their wisdom, are so many volumes behind social media, fantasy games, apps, etc., that they will never catch up. I see colleagues still trying to put coins into parking meters while a kid is paying with his smartphone.

Many countries have national curriculums, and the Education Ministries are given a sum which is then passed on down the line eventually ending up in a school for implementation. Those curriculums which were once worked on by very clever and sophisticated people are now struggling in this technological world. Change can be slow and national curriculums can easily end up a dinosaur in their relevance to the next generation. But yet the poor teacher has to implement it and will have a performance review based upon it and may be under the regime of merit pay.

Perhaps we should distinguish between policy and law. The law in most countries is that every child is entitled to basic formal education for a number of years. But government policies create inequities in implementation of those laws. It can also depend on who is in power at the time and if they allow policy to take over. Most countries manage to run reasonable schooling systems within the constraints of bureaucracies.

We have so many marginalized youth (teen parents, adjudicated youth, etc.) who need different supports to access mainstream culture in order to break the cycle of poverty. What role can education — in and out of school — play to support them?

In my experience the only way to actually bring a marginalized young person out of the cycle of poverty they live in is to provide wraparound services via the school. In one college, where I worked (the poorest in New Zealand with the highest Pasifika population at the time), we tried all manner of things to improve educational achievement. Most of it didn't work because students came to school hungry and there was no government-sponsored food program.

You cannot teach a hungry child. The family would often be in crisis and children were regularly bashed up by angry or drunk parents who had no work. Communicable diseases (yes, even in beautiful, peaceful New Zealand) were rife. Scabies, boils, rheumatic fever, tuberculosis — I saw it all. Try to teach a troubled child from that background the history of the Tudors. You may as well bark against thunder.

In this extreme case, food, pastoral care, healthcare, and education in that order became a solution to the problem of marginalized youth. It sounds easy, but I received a letter from the Minister of Education forbidding me to pay for food out of the "education" budget. I was publicly scolded by officials from the Department of Health for "making a scene" over a scabies outbreak affecting 70% of the 800 students as they said that "scabies didn't happen in winter." It most certainly did as I and other teachers got it. It became so bad (many students became infected and hospitalized) they considered calling in the military. The blind eye approach to "no scabies in winter" cost the country buckets of money to get it under control. The ministry response was real head-in-the-sand stuff. I solved the pastoral care problem by hiring retirees who were not brain dead at sixty-five but tired of classrooms full of kids who were too distressed to learn anything.

Eventually in my own little world I managed to shame, cajole, shout, stamp, etc., and I got all those things above that broke the cycle. It took me ten very long years and I probably neglected a lot of other things including my own children (who thankfully have grown up into amazing adults) but you need to ask the question — why did it have to be so difficult and take so long?

Once you get over that, education is filling that enquiring mind. And it is a joy to see the fruits of your labor.

SUSAN'S ONE GOOD QUESTION: I am still thinking about it!

WHAT ARE YOU WONDERING?

ANU WONDERS: How do we empower our students to keep their curiosity and growth mindset throughout their lives?

ANA WONDERS: How do we move "average students" to attain higher levels of success beyond being at top of class?

DERWIN WONDERS: Why are we missing the mark on diagnosing the problem with education reform? Do we have the wrong people asking the questions?

SUSAN WONDERS: I am still thinking about it!

When you think about multi-sector solutions, which sectors seem most related? What did you already know about collaboration for education outcomes that was challenged here?

As you reflect on your one good question —

- Think about your audience: Which voices were missing from this chapter? Who are the experts for your wondering?
- Think about your context: Which industries, sectors, or communities would contribute to your vision for a sustainable education for the most marginalized youth?
- Think about your timing: Are you trying to get clarity on what has occurred or on what could be?

CONCLUSION

"I am still thinking about it."
- Susan Baragwanath

Some of you may have reached this point in the book and have already crafted several good questions. Some of you have been talking back to the book, interrogating these experts in your head and giving examples of how your community is, or is not, aligned with their perspectives. Some of you are like Susan, and you are still thinking about it. Wherever you've landed after a first read is the right place to be.

As you keep thinking about your one good question, keep a few things in mind:

1. **Make mental space for unanticipated wonder:** In every interview, I was most engaged when the expert reached an inflection point that allowed them to go off script. As experts in our field, we often have a handful of talking points and poignant stories to share that get rehashed in every interview. *One Good Question* provided a different opportunity for the expert to let their mind wander. There was often a pause in our conversation followed by, "I hadn't thought about it like that. What if...." Our conversation made space for wonder. When was the last time you were in a conversation where you were not driving towards a predetermined outcome? When is the next time that you can make space for a conversation whose only agenda is wonder?

2. **Be clear about your known variables:** As I drafted and refined my one good question, I defined my known variables and unknown variables. Like in early algebra when problems introduce a mix of numbers and letters, the known variables helped me get clearer about the unknowns. I knew that young people were the beneficiaries of my question. Someone might talk about teacher practices, parent

perspectives, or local government, but all of that was a means to answer a question about their belief in young people. My second known variable was my hypothesis that funding reveals the strength of a belief system. Whether leaders wanted to address education funding from a micro or macro perspective was unknown to me. I didn't force leaders with less financial acumen to account for actuarial formulas in their state budgets. When leaders discussed programmatic investments or strategies, I was able to relate their examples to a budget decision that aligned with my wondering about financial implications. As you are thinking about your one good question, identify your known variables. Once you do that, it will be easier to engage a wide variety of people in the conversation.

3. **Figure out the motivation behind your wondering:** This is the part that requires some stillness, some introspection, and a lot of humility. Too often we are only committed to asking questions that prove our point. Read that sentence again. Without knowing anything about your wondering, I am fairly certain that if the goal of your question is to prove yourself right or prove someone else wrong, you are in the danger zone of having the right answer to the "wrong" question. Ask what is your motivation for asking your question. At the end of each chapter of this book, I've asked if you're trying to get clarity on something that has already occurred, or if you're envisioning something that is yet to be. I can't emphasize this enough. Do you know why you're trying to answer this question? True wonder requires opening yourself up to learning from different perspectives. It's difficult to do that if you've already answered the question in your mind.

And what about my one good question?

When I started this series, I couldn't have predicted what I would learn or where it would lead me professionally. One of the insights that emerged for me during these interviews is that most education leaders revealed that answers to their questions required some collaboration. A couple of years after starting my *One Good Question* interviews, I built my current nonprofit, Beloved Community, from that inspiration. We intentionally work across school, workforce, and housing systems because we believe that they are inextricably linked for sustainable community development. Another way that my one good question influenced my current work is transparency around resource and financial equity. During the interview series, our economic exploration usually included additional prompts like: If this is what you believe about youth and their capacity to lead, are you actually devoting resources to that end? If you or your systems are not funding that type of shift, why not? Those conversations impacted the ways that I built our model at Beloved Community, to include transparency around resource and financial equity as a part of sustainable development. The one good question that you ask may lead you in a new direction professionally, or help you develop an even deeper analysis for your current work. As you start questioning, stay open to the learning process.

I don't know what my next one good question will be, but I trust that it will lead me down the path to the right answers. What will your one good question be? Where will it lead you?

ACKNOWLEDGMENTS

I was born into a family of strong women. My grandmothers, Jessie Mae Ledet Celestine and Eva Morrison Broussard, and great-grandmother Olivia Goodie Ledet, raised us in different ways, different tongues, different dreams. So much of my inspiration in education and identity as a Black, Creole, French-speaking woman living in the diaspora came from them. To my parents, Rufus Broussard and Iris Olivia Celestine Broussard, thank you for supporting all of my professional projects, even when you didn't know exactly what they entailed. *"What do you do again?"* is a frequent conversation in our family and I'm okay with that. To Olivia Grace and Oscar Émil, my kids who have been on every adventure with me, thank you for being my muses, forever accountability partners and built-in market research. *"People are gonna pay you for that?"* If you don't have some honest kids in your life, I have a couple of junior consultants for your next project. And to my love, Kim, thank you for knowing when to ask me how the book was going and when to draw the bath, pour the wine, and trust the process.

Thank you to everyone that I interviewed for the series, even if our conversation doesn't appear in this book. I learned so much about the world, about new points of view, and about myself as a writer through this series. None of that could have been possible without each of you agreeing to share your stories with me. Some of the interviewees were friends or colleagues, some I had worked with closely, and some I had never met before. Some of the interviews were cold call emails — I pitched the blog idea, and they generously gave me an hour of their time. Two of the interviewees now serve on the board of directors of Beloved Community, my nonprofit. Many of the interviewees have gone on to start different organizations and bodies of work since we spoke. This book captures a moment in time in their professional careers and in the appendix, you can learn where their work has taken them today.

Ejaj Ahmad	Darren Isom	Chris Plutte
Amr AlMadani	Fabrice Jaumont	Ana Ponce
Susan Baraghwanath	Marcelo Knobel	Aylon Samouha
Karen Beeman	Noelle Lim	J.B. Schramm
Connie K. Chung	Vania Masias	Denese Shervington
Nicole de Beaufort	Ellen Moir	Derwin Sisnett
Mike DeGraff	Tony Monfiletto	Saku Tuominen
Michael Goetz	Kimberly Neal	Tom Vander Ark
Allan Golston	Ben Nelson	Dan Varner
Anna Hall	Kathy Padian	Susanna Williams
Zaki Hasan	Anu Passi-Rauste	John Wood
Alex Hernandez	Stefin Pasternak	Nicole Young
Peter Howe	Susan Patrick	

I'm grateful to the Eisenhower Fellowships program for giving me room and space to question. Thank you to my USA cohort (2014) and all of the leaders in Finland and New Zealand who opened their doors to me and my wonderings. I especially appreciate the Eisenhower Fellowships program staff for encouraging me to think bigger than my current work. I can't imagine how else I would have had the time for such deep personal, professional reflection and inspiration to write the original blog.

Many thanks to my krewe of advance readers: Alicia Robinson, Tricia DeGraff, Sara High, Deb Gordon, Christina Morado, Reva Broussard, Ruthie Epstein, Trish Adobea Tchume, Stephanie Malia Krauss, David Lewis, Kira Van Niel, and Rebecca Friedman. This book would not have been the same without your good questions.

To Kimberly Neal-Brannum and Stefin Pasternak, thank you for sharing your vision with me. I am more encouraged about the future of secondary education thanks to educators like you.

To Carlos Zamora, when we first met in that library in north St. Louis, I asked you one good question that brought us into a lifetime of family love. You were the first friend of this project, and your guidance was unparalleled. To the team at Cartel Strategies, thank you for making room to understand my work and translate it in the cover art and typography. To Lesly Washington for website development, you were one of my first collaborators on the book project and held my vision and timeline with such grace.

To my publisher, Fabrice Jaumont, without your vision, this book would have never come to be. Thank you for seeing the potential and voice in my writing.

ACKNOWLEDGEMENTS

Before starting this blog, I didn't consider myself a writer. I wrote as a part of my job, but I didn't identify myself as having a broader message or broader audience for my work. I'm thankful to Michael B. Horn for encouraging me to write and featuring me in his Forbes column[49]. Dr. Lisa M. Dorner was my research partner for a decade (and is still waiting for me to start that PhD program) and she helped me honor the relationship between practice, research, and writing. Since our undergraduate days, Jarvis DeBerry has been one of my favorite poets, columnists and writers. When he started reading my blog, I was a little nervous. Not only did Jarvis appreciate my voice, he promoted the blog voluntarily and encouraged me to keep writing. When I started considering turning the blog into a book, Jarvis was the first call I made. He had just published *I Feel to Believe*, a collection of his columns for The Times-Picayune. I appreciated his guidance on the business process and how to editorialize my own work.

Earlier, I mentioned being a student in this Wonder Why program in third grade. I didn't have many teachers in my life who honored questioning; in fact most teachers bristled at my smart mouth and incessant whys. I'm thankful that I was able to get validation for my questioning nature at such a young age. To all of the teachers who encourage their students to question — to question their own beliefs, to question the text, to question the curriculum, to question adult perspectives, to question policies and rules — this book is for you. Especially when your school leadership or administration doesn't value interrogation as a learning tool, remember that questioning is at the core of critical analysis for students at every age.

Finally, to everyone who read, subscribed to, liked, or commented on the original blog series, thank you for making space for *One Good Question* in your lives.

---

[49] Horn, Michael B. "Finland Offers Lessons for Building Student, Teacher Agency." Forbes Magazine. August 13, 2015. https://www.forbes.com/sites/michaelhorn/2015/08/13/finland-offers-lessons-for-building-student-teacher-agency

ABOUT RHONDA

"...ideas glow so brightly, they illuminate a path for the rest of us."
- St. Louis Luminary, St. Louis Magazine 2009

Education is Rhonda's social justice issue, and she has been a leader in diversity and international education initiatives throughout her career in public education. Rhonda Broussard founded Beloved Community to create sustainable paths to racial and economic equity. Her vision for Beloved Community is informed by her leadership in diverse-by-design schools and Rev. Dr. Martin Luther King Jr.'s goal, "to create a beloved community and this will require a qualitative change in our souls as well as a quantitative change in our lives." In 2016, she founded The Ochosi Group, an education consulting group that supports schools and education nonprofits to transform their practices (growth, replication, new program development) and align adult culture with key beliefs for teaching and learning.

In 2007, she founded St. Louis Language Immersion Schools (SLLIS). SLLIS is an intentionally diverse school community and was the first public school in the US to offer this rigorous academic model to a majority minority student population and socioeconomically diverse student population. Under Rhonda's leadership, the first three schools in the network became International Baccalaureate World Authorized Schools, and SLLIS achieved an Adequate Yearly Progress (AYP) of 92%, equivalent to Accreditation with Distinction from the Department of Elementary and Secondary Education. Rhonda served as President of SLLIS until June 2015.

Rhonda is a Pahara-Aspen Institute Fellow and a member of the Aspen Global Leaders Network. She is a 2014 recipient of the Eisenhower Fellowship for International Leadership. During her fellowship she studied whole system education reform and teacher education practices in Finland and New Zealand. Rhonda serves on the Board of Directors of PROMO Missouri and the Missouri Charter Public School Association. Rhonda has received numerous recognitions, including 2008 30 Leaders 30 Years by Breakthrough Collaborative; 2009 St. Louis

Luminary by St. Louis Magazine; 2010 Buzz List by ALIVE Magazine; 2010 YMCA Strong Kids Zealot by The Monsanto Family YMCA; 2012 Diverse Business Leader by St. Louis Business Journal; 2013 Outstanding African American Citizen by Gateway Classic; 2013 Social Sector Excellence Award by St. Louis New Leaders Council; and 2015 People Who Inspire by Delux Magazine.

Rhonda Broussard is a native of Lafayette, Louisiana. Rhonda has taught French in public schools in New York City, Connecticut, California and St. Louis and has earned National Board Certification, the most prestigious teaching credential in the United States. Rhonda completed her undergraduate studies in French and Secondary Education at Washington University in St. Louis and a Master of Arts degree in French Studies from New York University's Institute of French Studies. Growing up in Louisiana, she was inspired by the idea of the francophone world and has dedicated herself to continuing to explore the connections between francophone regions. As a result, in addition to learning French since childhood, she has studied and conducted research in metropolitan France, Cameroon and Martinique. Rhonda began her education reform career as a teenage staff member with the Breakthrough Collaborative in New Orleans, Kansas City and San Francisco.

Rhonda currently serves as chair of the board of directors of EdNavigator and treasurer of Dat School Agile Learning Center. She also serves on the board of directors for both Diverse Charter School Coalition and the Krewe of Themis. Previously, Rhonda has served on the board of Missouri Charter Public School Association, PROMO — Missouri's LGBT Advocacy Leader, and Campus YMCA-YWCA. Rhonda lives with her partner Kim and two children Olivia and Oscar in her native Louisiana. She studies, performs, and occasionally teaches dances from the African diaspora.

INTERVIE BIOGRAPHIES

Ejaj Ahmad is founder and president of Bangladesh Youth Leadership Center (BYLC). He developed the idea for BYLC while he was a graduate student at Harvard University, and established the social enterprise in Bangladesh in 2009 with the vision of creating a more just, prosperous, and inclusive society by training the next generation of leaders. Over the past ten years, he has overseen the organization's rapid growth — to date, there are 4,500 BYLC alumni, many of whom have gone on to leadership roles across Bangladesh and abroad. BYLC today is disrupting the higher education landscape in Bangladesh by providing world-class leadership training through physical and blended courses, tackling youth unemployment by influencing government policies, connecting youth to jobs through physical and online networks, and instilling in them values of public service and community engagement.

Furthermore, BYLC is creating the next generation of high-impact entrepreneurs through incubation and investment support. For his work, Ejaj received numerous national and international awards and fellowships, most notably the Ashoka Fellowship, Eisenhower Fellowship, and Harvard Kennedy School's Rising Star Award. He received his MPP from Harvard University and his MA with honors in economics from St. Andrews University.

Dr. Susan Baragwanath works as an independent consultant. She was a career secondary school teacher and administrator who taught internationally. Susan is the founder of He Huarahi Tamariki Schools, Māori for "a chance for children." Her program plan was to provide basic formal education and training for teen parents to graduate from high school. These include high-quality preschools. The highly acclaimed schools were honored and became models, replicated in more than fifty locations around New Zealand.

Susan is an authority in women's leadership. She has had extensive international experience in education and criminal justice and has mentored dozens of women from all walks of life. She has recently organized two international strategic programs for women's leadership in London, chaired international search committees for outstanding women leaders, and is a Distinguished Eisenhower Fellow. In 2005, she received the highest academic award in the Humanities, Doctor of Letters, for education reform of school age mothers in New Zealand.

Karen Beeman, co-founder of the Center for Teaching Biliteracy, is an education consultant whose specialty is biliteracy and bilingual education. Karen's professional experience includes working as a bilingual teacher, principal of a dual-language school in the city of Chicago, and as a professor at the University of Illinois at Chicago and at National Louis University. The area that has most captured Karen's passion and work is biliteracy, how to teach children how to read and write in two languages at the same time. As a professional developer, Karen works at the national level providing training for teachers and principals and she also collaborates with the Illinois Resource Center. A simultaneous bilingual born and raised in Mexico City, Karen is co-author, along with Cheryl Urow, of the book *Teaching for Biliteracy: Strengthening Bridges between Languages* (Caslon Publishing, 2013) and is co-founder of the Center for Teaching for Biliteracy, an on-line forum for supporting and connecting educators who teach for biliteracy: www.TeachingForBiliteracy.com

Como una bilingüe simultánea, nacida y criada en México, que aprendió a leer y a escribir en español y en inglés desde la primaria hasta la preparatoria, Karen se identifica con muchos de los estudiantes bilingües en los EE.UU., y busca apoyar a los educadores a que desarrollen el potencial de todos sus estudiantes para que sobresalgan académicamente. Su pasión hacia la lectoescritura bilingüe ha nacido de sus experiencias personales y profesionales en donde su biculturalismo y su bilingüismo siempre han sido enriquecidos.

Nicole de Beaufort is a social entrepreneur based in Detroit, Michigan. Nicole is an architect of imagination. She co-designs blueprints for social change that transform the way people consider an issue or make decisions that affect the public good. She is relentlessly attracted to making a difference.

Nicole named her third company EarlyWorks because it describes her approach to the world so well: show up early or on time, do good work, rinse and repeat. Nicole is a leader in strategic communications ranging from global affairs to block-level outreach and engagement. Nicole has committed more than twenty years to facilitating social change while serving in leadership positions within nonprofits, foundations, and cross-sector initiatives.

A graduate of Williams College, Nicole is a 2013 Marshall Memorial Fellow, a 2018 Goldman Sachs 10,000 Small Businesses graduate, a 2019 AltMBA alum, and in 2020 received a Public Leadership Credential from Harvard University's Kennedy School of Government.

Nicole serves on the executive committees of Jefferson East, Inc. and CitizenDetroit. She is a past board president of 826Michigan. In 2014, she co-founded the Detroit Women's Leadership Network.

Connie K. Chung is a Design Strategy Fellow with Foster America, designing an integrated support system for foster youth that enables them to thrive. In this work, she is continuing to pursue her lifelong interest in knitting research, practice, and policy to build the capacities of organizations and people to work collaboratively toward providing a relevant, rigorous, meaningful education for all children that not only supports their individual growth but also the growth of their communities. She is the former associate director of the Global Education Innovation Initiative at the Harvard Graduate School of Education, a multi-institution global research collaborative, a former consultant to the OECD, and a former foster parent. She is the co-editor and contributor of books about community organizing, curriculum, teacher professional development, and innovations in education. A former high school English literature teacher, she was nominated by her students for teaching awards. Connie received her BA, EdM's, and EdD from Harvard University and her dissertation analyzed the individual and organizational factors that facilitated people from diverse ethnic, religious, and socio-economic class backgrounds to work together to build a better community.

Michael DeGraff is a senior implementation specialist at PowerSchool. In his previous work at the UTeach Institute, he coordinated the Instruction

Program Review process for all UTeach Partner Sites as well as supporting instructors to implement the nine UTeach courses. Michael has been a part of UTeach since 2001, first as an undergraduate student at UT Austin (BA Mathematics with Secondary Teaching Option, 2005), then as a graduate student (MA Mathematics Education, 2007), and finally as a Master Teacher with UKanTeach at the University of Kansas. He was also instrumental in launching Austin Maker Education.

Dr. Fred Genesee is professor emeritus in the Psychology Department at McGill University, Montreal. He is interested in basic issues related to language learning, representation, and use in bilinguals and in applied issues related to second language teaching, learning, and assessment. He has conducted extensive research on alternative forms of bilingual/ immersion education for language minority and language majority students, the academic development of at-risk students in bilingual programs, language acquisition in typically-developing and at-risk preschool bilingual children, and internationally-adopted children. He has published numerous articles in scientific journals, professional books and magazines and is the author of sixteen books on bilingualism. He is the recipient of the Canadian Psychology Association Gold Medal Award, Paul Pimsler Award for Research in Foreign Language Education, Canadian Psychological Association Award for Distinguished Contributions to Community or Public Service, California Association for Bilingual Education Award for Promoting Bilingualism and the le prix Adrien-Pinard.

Allan Golston is the president of the United States Program at the Bill & Melinda Gates Foundation. He leads the Bill & Melinda Gates Foundation's five areas of strategy, policy and advocacy, and operations of a $600 million domestic program with $3.8 billion portfolio under management: K-12 Education, Post-Secondary Education, Technology Access, Special Initiatives, and Family Homelessness, Early Childhood Learning, and Community Grants in Washington State.

In addition to his work at the foundation, Allan also sits on a number of boards (University of Washington Medicine, Seattle University, Charter School Growth Fund, MOM Brands). Allan is a lifetime member of the British-American Project and has previously been an active board member for Global Alliance for Vaccines and Immunization (GAVI), New Futures, Make-A-Wish Foundation of Alaska and Washington, Philanthropy Northwest, and the Public Library of Science. Allan is a resource council member for both the Rainier Scholars program and the Robert Woods Johnson Commission to Build a Healthier America, on the advisory committee for the Northwest African American Museum in Seattle and is on the Resource Council for the Smithsonian National Museum of African American History and Culture in Washington DC. Allan is also actively involved in the HOPE Street Bipartisan Commission and the INROADS Alumni Association. He is a member of the 2009 class of Henry Crown Fellows at the Aspen Institute.

Dr. Michael Goetz is the executive director of Regional Services and Education Center (RSEC). Clients include the Bill & Melinda Gates Foundation, National Center for Innovation in Education, Council for Better Education, Foundation for Child Development, National Academy of Education, School District of Palm Beach County, Allovue, Picus Odden and Associates, and several legislative and gubernatorial committees.

In addition to managing the day-to-day operations of RSEC, Michael leads projects related to educational policy and school finance research. He has worked with academics and policymakers to analyze fiscal data and develop models for PK-12 school finance equity and adequacy in Kentucky, North Dakota, Maine, Texas, Arkansas, Washington, Wisconsin, Wyoming, and Arizona. Michael has also performed analyses of school-based resource allocation and restructuring in Alaska, Hawaii, Kentucky, Missouri, New Jersey, Washington, Wisconsin, and Wyoming.

Before focusing on school finance policy, Michael was a researcher with the Consortium for Policy Research in Education (CPRE) at the University of Wisconsin-Madison. Prior to joining CPRE, he managed K-8 educational centers for Score Learning, Inc. in New York and taught middle school math and science in Kansas City.

Michael received a BA in Educational Studies from Washington University in St. Louis and a PhD in Educational Leadership and Policy Analysis at University of Wisconsin-Madison. He received a Wisconsin-

Spencer Doctoral Research Program Fellowship, a dissertation grant from the American Educational Research Association (AERA), and the American Education Finance Association (AEFA) New Scholar Award.

Anna Hall is a seasoned educator with experience developing and leading a range of institutional, state, and national initiatives. As a founding teacher of a highly successful small New York City public high school, she collaborated to design and build an innovative and rigorous secondary program for students in the South Bronx — and then, as principal, she led the school's expansion and redesigned its academic programs. Prior to teaching, Anna spent nearly a decade working as a writer, researcher, and project manager in a range of policy, politics, and technology firms. Anna has supported public school design work with Springpoint: Partners in School Design and Transcend Education. Anna holds a BA from the South Carolina Honors College at the University of South Carolina, and an MS in teaching from Fordham University. She is a graduate of both the New York City Teaching Fellows Program and the New York City Leadership Academy.

Zaki Hasan is a nonprofit organization expert with twenty years of experience of working with seven international non-governmental organizations (NGOs) and one Bangladeshi national non-governmental organization. The experience includes about twelve years of top management experience with two international NGOs and one national NGO of Bangladesh. Zaki has vast experience in program innovations, proposal development, fund mobilization, monitoring, project management including extensive experience of financial and HR management, program reporting and documentation, research and program evaluations, audit and compliance management, etc. in the education, health and nutrition sub-sectors. He is a USA President Eisenhower Fellow and UK Government International Leadership awardee. Zaki is currently pursuing PhD in Public Policy in the University of Saskatchewan.

Kaya Henderson is the CEO of Reconstruction, a technology company delivering a K-12 supplemental curriculum that situates Black people, culture, and contributions in an authentic, identity-affirming way, so that students of all backgrounds benefit from a more complete understanding of our shared history and society.

She is also the co-host of Pod Save the People, and leads Kaya Henderson Consulting. She is perhaps best known for serving as chancellor of DC Public Schools from 2010-2016. Her tenure was marked by consecutive years of enrollment growth, an increase in graduation rates, improvements in student satisfaction and teacher retention, increases in Advanced Placement (AP) participation and pass rates, and the greatest growth of any urban district on the National Assessment of Education Progress (NAEP) over multiple years.

Kaya's career began as a middle school Spanish teacher in the South Bronx, through Teach For America. She went on to work as a recruiter, national admissions director, and DC executive director for Teach for America. Kaya then served as the vice president of strategic partnerships at The New Teacher Project (TNTP) until she began her tenure at DCPS as deputy chancellor in 2007. She most recently led the Global Learning Lab for Community Impact at Teach For All, supporting educators in more than 50 countries.

A native of Mt. Vernon, NY, Kaya graduated from Mt. Vernon Public Schools. She received her Bachelor's degree in International Relations and her Master of Arts in Leadership from Georgetown University, as well as honorary doctoral degrees from Georgetown and Trinity University. Her board memberships include The Aspen Institute, Curriculum Associates, Robin Hood NYC, and Teach For America, and she is the co-founder of Education Leaders of Color (EdLoC).

Alejandro ("Alex") Hernandez is the tenth president of Champlain College. Alex was born to a family of public educators in Stockton, California. His parents journeyed from Mexico and the Philippines, and, at each step of the way, education brought opportunity — through skilled trades, nursing certificates, education credentials and degrees. These experiences shaped Alex's belief that career-focused education can change lives and help communities thrive.

Before Champlain College Alex served as the dean of the School of Continuing and Professional Studies (SCPS) and vice provost of Online

Learning at University of Virginia. At UVA, Alex championed access, affordability, and opportunity through its bachelor's completion, professional certificate, and graduate programs. Alex helped SCPS enroll its largest undergraduate class in school history, launch its first master's degree, and pursue a strategy that combined in-demand digital skills with the human skills needed for long-term career success. He also taught undergraduate courses in entrepreneurship (SCPS) and education innovation (School of Education and Human Development).

Before joining UVA, Alex worked for the Charter School Growth Fund, a national education foundation, where he built the nonprofit's Innovative Schools practice, one of the largest efforts in the country focused on personalized learning and career readiness. Alex began his education career teaching high school mathematics in South Los Angeles. He later became an administrator for Portland Public Schools in Oregon and then an area superintendent for Aspire Public Schools in California. Prior to entering the field of education, he worked at Steamboat Ventures, Disney's venture capital arm, and at J.P. Morgan. Alex has an MBA and MA in Education from Stanford University and a BA from Claremont McKenna College. He is a moderator for the Aspen Global Leadership Network and a Pahara Institute fellow.

Peter Howe is head of school at Somersfield Academy in Bermuda. Previously, Peter served as principal of UWC Atlantic, the founding school of the United World College movement. Prior to joining UWC Atlantic in March 2017, Peter was head of college at UWC Maastricht for five years following a seven-year tenure at UWC Adriatic in Italy, four of which as the head of the college.

Peter brings an eclectic background to his position. Following an undergraduate degree in finance and economics and two years working at Procter & Gamble in his native Canada, he returned to study graduate art and architectural history for seven years before embarking on his teaching career.

Darren Isom is a partner in The Bridgespan Group's San Francisco office. He first joined the firm as a consultant in 2007, left as a manager in 2014 and returned as a partner in 2019. During his earlier tenure with Bridgespan, Darren was engaged with a diverse array of cases and was consistently lauded for building deep, enduring client relationships, helping clients develop bold yet pragmatic strategies, and his commitment to amplifying community voice and engagement in developing and leading innovative, high-impact youth and community programs, practices, and philanthropy.

After leaving Bridgespan in 2014, Darren was the founder and executive director of the Memphis Music Initiative (MMI), an ambitious five-year, $20M grantmaking and community arts development initiative. He led efforts to use targeted investments and programmatic offerings to strengthen youth and community music engagement activities for low-income, Black, and Latino youth and communities. MMI leverages the city's powerful musical legacy to develop a vibrant music and arts ecosystem for the city's culturally rich, but historically underserved communities, and grew to impact 4,500 youth, fifty schools, 100 musicians and artists, ten neighborhoods, and fifteen community organizations. It has also sponsored research to create a national conversation on the importance of community engagement and inclusion, disruptive philanthropy, and the powerful role of arts investments in driving equitable, high-impact community outcomes. To launch and lead the organization, Darren built strategic relationships with arts organizations, musicians, schools, funders, community, public, and private groups; built the team, including a diverse and inclusive board and twenty staff; and developed a robust infrastructure for delivering results in Memphis and the Mid-South, a particularly racialized region.

Before Bridgespan he worked as the art, design, and public programming director for Times Square Alliance, planning and implementing programming for public art and performance initiatives throughout the Times Square District. Prior to working at Times Square Alliance, Darren served as vice president of programs for Groundwork, a start-up youth services organization in East New York, Brooklyn, helping young people in underserved communities develop their strengths and skills through experiential learning and enrichment programs.

A seventh generation New Orleans native, Darren is a graduate of Howard University, Institut d'Études Politiques de Paris, and Columbia

Business School's Institute for Nonprofit Management. An activist for disconnected youth and LGBT communities of color, he has served as an advisor to the leaders of several Bay Area, Southeast US, and national foundations. He currently serves on the board of Beloved Community of New Orleans, Collage Dance Collective of Memphis, Springboard to Opportunities in Jackson, MS, and the National Guild for Community Arts Education.

Fabrice Jaumont is a scholar-practitioner, award-winning author, non-profit leader, and education advisor based in New York. He currently serves as education attaché for the Embassy of France to the United States, a Research Fellow at Fondation Maison des Sciences de l'Homme in Paris, and an adjunct professor at New York University and Baruch College – The City University of New York. He is president of the Center for the Advancement of Languages, Education, and Communities, a nonprofit publishing organization with a focus on multilingualism, cross-cultural understanding, and the empowerment of linguistic communities. He has published five books, including *The Bilingual Revolution: The Future of Education Is in Two Languages*, which provides guidance and advice for parents and educators who want to create a dual-language program in their own school. Fabrice holds a PhD in Comparative and International Education from New York University.

Marcelo Knobel was the twelfth rector of the University of Campinas (Unicamp), in Brazil, where he is a full professor of physics. He held other leadership roles, including executive director of the Unicamp Exploratory Science Museum, vice-rector for undergraduate programs, vice-president of the Brazilian Physics Society and executive director of the Brazilian Nanotechnology National Laboratory (LNNano). Marcelo has already published more than 250 scientific papers, in addition to numerous opinion pieces in both national and international newspapers and magazines. He is the editor-in-chief of the Journal of Magnetism and Magnetic Materials (Elsevier). Marcelo is an Eisenhower Fellow (2007), Fellow of the John Simon Guggenheim Memorial Foundation (2009) and Lemann Fellow (2015). He is member (elect) of the Governing Council of the Magna Charta Observatory.

Noelle Lim is regional head of Corporate Communications at Maybank Investment Banking Group. She has had a long career in business affairs communications serving as a presenter and producer on BFM 89.9 The Business Station, executive director of BFM-Edge B School, and a contributing editor to Forbes Asia. Noelle started her career as an analyst with Arthur Andersen, Securities Commission Malaysia, and OSK Investment Bank (now RHB).

In 2020 Noelle founded Kindermind Center, a social-purpose organization that aims to transform minds and promote resilience and compassion through accessible, evidence-based mindfulness training rooted in rigorous standards of teaching. Noelle completed a Bsc of Accounting at University of Hull, completed an Asian Journalism Fellowship at Nanyang Technological University Singapore, is a Fellow at ICAEW, and is an Eisenhower Fellow.

Vania Masías is the founding director of Angeles D1, where she has produced choreography and musicals. Vania is a professional ballerina and a social entrepreneur. She performed as a principal dancer for the Municipal Ballet of Lima, acting in main roles of the classical repertoire. Later on, she performed as a modern dancer in Europe and the Caribbean, danced at the Irish National Ballet and was selected to perform for Cirque du Soleil. Finally, she decided to return to Lima to start Angeles D1, a self-sustaining social enterprise that provides artistic dance training for marginalized kids who are thereby transformed into professional dancers.

She is an ambassador of Marca Perú, and has won the Synacyd Social Innovation award, the Indecopi Institutional award 2012, and the Esteban Campodónico award for service to society. GQ magazine named her as inspiration person of the year 2012, while Trome newspaper included her among the eleven most notable Peruvians of 2012. The City of Lima named her a Distinguished Citizen in 2009. She is member of the consulting council of the Ministry of Culture and member of the Board of Peru2021.

Ellen Moir founded New Teacher Center in 1998 to scale high-quality teacher induction services to a national audience. NTC has reached more than 250,000 teachers across the country. Ellen stepped down as CEO August 2018, and is currently an independent educational consultant.

Ellen is widely recognized for her work in beginning teacher development and school reform. She has extensive experience in public education, having previously served as director of teacher education at the University of California at Santa Cruz and worked as a bilingual teacher. Ellen has been named the 2014 Brock International Prize in Education Laureate, became a Pahara-Aspen Education Fellow in 2013, an Ashoka Fellow in 2011, and is a recipient of the 2011 Skoll Award for Social Entrepreneurship. Other major awards include the 2013 NewSchools Venture Fund Organization of the Year Award; 2010 Civic Ventures Purpose Prize Fellow; 2008 National Staff Development Council Contribution to the Field award; the 2008 Full Circle Fund Impact Award; the Harold W. McGraw, Jr. 2005 Prize in Education; and the 2003 California Council on Teacher Education Distinguished Teacher Educator Award. Ellen has also co-authored many publications, including Keys to the Classroom and Keys to the Secondary Classroom, New Teacher Mentoring: Hopes and Promise for Improving Teacher Effectiveness, and Blended Coaching: Skills and Strategies to Support Principal Development.

For more than twenty years, she has pioneered innovative approaches to new teacher development, research on new teacher practice, and the design and administration of teacher induction programs. She is recognized as a passionate advocate for our nation's teachers and for the students they teach.

Tony Monfiletto is the executive director of Future Focused Education. Tony Monfiletto's family has a long history in New Mexico and his Chicano heritage informs his vision. Tony has worked in education since 1990. He has been a leader in establishing the context for a network of schools in his hometown of Albuquerque, NM, and a broader vision for schools to be the catalyst for creating healthier and more prosperous communities.

In 2008, Tony began working on ACE Leadership High School, the first in a network of the next generation of career-focused schools that are designed to serve students that are off-track to graduation or are no longer attending school. There are now four schools in the Leadership Schools Network which are committed to providing "the best education for the students who need it the most."

He is emerging as a leader in equity conversations across the country. His belief in local wisdom and the inherent value of young people and their lived experience frames his approach to the most complex and seemingly intractable problems we face.

Kimberly Neal is founder and executive director of Believe Schools. Prior to developing Believe Schools, Kim held several leadership positions at KIPP DC including managing director of secondary education. Her responsibilities included coaching and supporting middle school leaders, supporting network-wide curriculum initiatives, and implementing strong culture systems. Previously, Kimberly was the founding principal for Muchin College Prep, a campus of Noble Network. Muchin has consistently ranked as a Tier 1+ High School and is among the highest performing non-selective schools in the city of Chicago. Kimberly also served as a turnaround school leader for a year at AIM Academy, KIPP DC. There, she was instrumental in stabilizing the school and creating a culture of identity and academic achievement.

Kimberly earned her BA in Psychology and Criminal Justice from Alabama Agricultural and Mechanical University, an MSW from Washington University, St. Louis, and an MEd from Teachers College-Columbia University. Kimberly has participated in the 2011 Chinese Bridge Delegation, National Principal Supervisors Cohort at Relay Graduate School of Education, and School Design Camp for NewSchools Venture Fund. Kimberly is a Cambiar Catalyst Fellow and a MindTrust Innovation Fellow.

Ben Nelson started Minerva in 2011 with the goal of nurturing critical wisdom for the sake of the world through a systematic and evidence-based approach to learning. Over the past ten years, Ben has built Minerva Schools at Keck Graduate Institute into the most selective and effective university in the United States, and has developed a business to share Minerva's unique approach with other like-minded institutions, corporations and governments.

Prior to Minerva, Ben spent more than ten years at Snapfish, where he helped build the company from startup to the world's largest personal publishing service. With over forty-two million transactions across twenty-two countries, nearly five times greater than its closest competitor, Snapfish is among the top e-commerce services in the world. Serving as CEO from 2005 through 2010, Ben began his tenure at Snapfish by leading the company's sale to Hewlett-Packard for $300 million.

Ben's passion for reforming education was first sparked at the University of Pennsylvania's Wharton School, where he received a BS in Economics. After creating a blueprint for curricular reform in his first year, the principles from which he drew to frame Minerva, Nelson went on to become the chair of the Student Committee on Undergraduate Education (SCUE), a pedagogical think tank that is the oldest and only non-elected student government body at the University of Pennsylvania.

Kathleen Padian joined TenSquare as a partner in 2015 and opened its second office in New Orleans, Louisiana. Kathleen has twenty-five years of experience working in the public education sector. She most recently served as the deputy superintendent for the Orleans Parish School Board where she created the authorizing office for charter schools and designed the first accountability framework. In that role she was also responsible for the office of facilities where she managed more than $400 million in school construction and renovation projects. Prior to OPSB, Kathleen founded the New Orleans School Facility Project which was funded by the Walton Family Foundation and was the only organization to convene stakeholders around the massive reconstruction of New Orleans public schools following the devastation following Hurricane Katrina. Kathleen has also served as vice president of Building Hope (DC) as the national director of development for New Leaders (New York), as strategic investments director for Fight for Children (DC) and was responsible for the multi-site expansion of St. Coletta of Greater Washington, raising more than $12 million and directly managing the strategic planning for its new 100,000-square-foot facility in the District of Columbia.

Kathleen began her career as a high school English teacher in Connecticut and as a special education teacher for children with severe and profound disabilities at St. Coletta. Kathleen holds degrees in English from the University of Connecticut, a Master of Arts in Teaching from Quinnipiac University and earned special education certification at the Curry School of Education at the University of Virginia where she also studied Educational Leadership.

Anu Passi-Rauste is partner and head of business development at Headai, a Finnish technology company. Anu has twenty years of experience in edtech business and learning solutions. She is responsible for building the market intelligence, business growth, customer success and scaling sales. Anu was an Eisenhower Fellow in 2014.

Stefin Pasternak is co-founder and head teacher of Living School. Stefin has been an educator in the New Orleans area since 2008 including reading, writing, and the culinary arts to students K-12. A New School Creation Fellow at High Tech High, his passion is seeking right relationship with all our relations by creating unique, project-based experiences for students like a student-run restaurant and multi-genre autoethnographies. He loves anything physical and outdoors, permaculture, growing, foraging, and preparing food, building structures, writing, music, games, and spending time with young people — especially his two sons.

Susan Patrick is the president and CEO of Aurora Institute, a national nonprofit organization with the mission to drive the transformation of education systems and accelerate the advancement of breakthrough policies and practices to ensure high-quality learning for all. She is the former director of the Office of Educational Technology at the US Department of Education. Prior, Susan served as legislative liaison for Governor Hull from Arizona. She served as legislative staff on Capitol Hill. She is a Pahara-Aspen Institute Fellow and an Eisenhower Fellow. She was awarded the AECT System Change Leader Award 2020 for making significant contributions to the evolution of learning, demonstrating systems thinking and positive impact aligned to future-focused education.

Chris Plutte is managing director of the Bezos Family Foundation. An entrepreneur and leader in education, media, and conflict resolution, he co-founded Global Nomads Group in 1998 and led the organization for more than a decade. Prior to rejoining GNG in 2010, Chris opened and directed Search for Common Ground and was chief of party on initiatives for the Great Lakes region of the DRC, Burundi, and Rwanda. At both organizations, he managed project and program development. A speaker on media, youth, and conflict, Chris has appeared on "The Today Show," CNN and NPR, and in Education Week and Chronicles of Philanthropy. He is a Pahara Fellow and a member of Aspen Global Leadership Network.

Dr. Ana F. Ponce is the executive director of Great Public Schools Now. Most recently, Ana was the chief executive officer of Camino Nuevo Charter Academy, a network of six charter schools and an early education center serving more than 3,600 students in central Los Angeles. Her accomplishments prompted Forbes Magazine in 2011 to name her one of the top seven most powerful educators in the world.

Ana is the youngest daughter of Mexican immigrants and the first in her family to graduate college. She earned a full scholarship to Middlebury College in Vermont, a world away from Pico Union, the neighborhood where she grew up. Her first teaching job was a Teach for America assignment at a public school in South L.A. After three years in the classroom, she landed a fellowship at Columbia University's Teachers College in New York, where she earned a master's degree in bilingual education.

Determined to close the achievement and opportunity gaps for low-income minority students, she returned to Los Angeles and helped open the first independent charter school in South L.A., where she taught for seven years before joining Camino Nuevo in 2001. At Camino Nuevo, she found herself working with families in the neighborhood where she grew up, investing them and their children in being College Ready, College Bound.

During her tenure as CEO, Ana was instrumental in driving the success of the organization and championing high quality educational opportunities for kids. She has demonstrated that schools comprised almost entirely of English learners, in some of the city's poorest and densest neighborhoods, can achieve extraordinary results and serve as models of excellence.

Ana holds a second master's degree from the University of California, Los Angeles and a doctorate in educational leadership from Loyola Marymount University. A veteran of the charter schools movement in California, she serves on several boards and committees, including the Board of the California Charter Schools Association, the Educators of

Color (EdLoc) Leadership Committee, the L.A. County Commission on Local Government Services, and UnidosUS.

Aylon Samouha is a co-founder of Transcend Education Group. Prior to co-founding Transcend, Aylon was an independent designer providing strategy and design services to education organizations, schools, and foundations. Most recently, Aylon has been leading the "Greenfield" school model design for the Achievement First Network, which was piloted in the 2015-16 school year. He also led the field research for Charter School Growth Fund and the Clay Christensen Institute for the 2014 publication, "Schools and Software: What's Now, What's Next." In 2013, Aylon pioneered the Chicago Breakthrough Schools Fellowship in conjunction with New Schools for Chicago, NGLC, and the Broad Foundation.

Aylon served as chief schools officer at Rocketship Education, leading the highest-performing network of low-income schools in the state of California, designing the academic model and blended learning approach, and growing the network from three to seven schools. Aylon also spent several years as a senior vice president at Teach For America, leading pre-service institutes and in-service support for corps members in their two-year teaching commitments during a period of growth from 4,000 to 8,000 corps members.

After graduating from Columbia University with a BA in English, Aylon spent the first part of his career at Score Educational Centers working with families, leading K-8 learning centers and ultimately managing more than sixty branches across the country.

J.B. Schramm is founder and managing partner of Grove Social Impact Partners, a national partnership of leading social entrepreneurs catalyzing bold, cross-sector, impact initiatives. J.B. formerly founded and led New Profit's $25 milion Learn to Earn initiative to help learners achieve economic mobility by weaving work and study together, incubating the Future of Work Grand Challenge, Postsecondary Innovation for Equity (PIE) fund, and the College Success Award. Forbes named J.B. to its "Impact 30" list of top global social entrepreneurs for his work leading College Summit (now called PeerForward), the nonprofit J.B. founded in the basement of a low-income housing development in

1995. In 2010, College Summit was recognized by President Obama with a portion of his Nobel Peace Prize, and by the US Chamber of Commerce as the nation's top corporate/nonprofit partnership.

Selected as the US Social Entrepreneur of the Year at the World Economic Forum (2007), J.B. is the recipient of honorary doctorates from Regis University and the Université Catholique de Louvain (Belgium). Yale University honored J.B. with the inaugural Yale-Jefferson Award in 2012, and Harvard Divinity School awarded him the First Decade Award in 2000. He is a fellow of the Manhattan Institute, Aspen Institute, Skoll Foundation and Ashoka. J.B. has been published and highlighted by numerous media outlets including The New York Times, The Washington Post, People, and the Consumer Electronics Show.

Dr. Denese Shervington has an intersectional career in public health and academic psychiatry. She is the president of The Institute of Women and Ethnic Studies (IWES), a community-based translational public health institute in New Orleans. She is also the chair of Psychiatry at Charles R. Drew University. Denese has held clinical professorships in the Departments of Psychiatry at Columbia University and Tulane University. A graduate of New York University School of Medicine, she also received a Masters of Public Health in Population Studies and Family Planning from Tulane University School of Public Health. She completed her residency in Psychiatry at the University of California San Francisco and is certified by the American Board of Psychiatry and Neurology. A Fellow of the American Psychiatry Association, in 2018 she received the Award for Excellence in Service and Advocacy, prior to which she received the Jeanne Spurlock Minority award. Denese is also a member of the American College of Psychiatrists.

In July 2019, Denese testified before the Congress of the United States House of Representatives' Committee on Oversight and Reform on Childhood Trauma. She also co-chairs the New Orleans City Council (R-18-344) Children Youth Planning Board Task Force on Childhood Trauma. In 2020, Denese was appointed as a member of the Scientific Board of the Centre for Society and Mental Health at Kings College, London. She has authored several papers in peer-reviewed journals addressing health disparities, the social determinants of health and resilience in underserved communities. Her recent publication is *Healing Is the Revolution*, a guide to healing from historical, intergenerational, interpersonal, and community trauma. She also hosts the podcast "Healing Is the Revolution," in which her guests share and explore their healing journey through their traumas.

Derwin Sisnett is the founder and partner of Maslow Development Inc. (Maslow), a real estate and community development firm that advises, designs, and develops mixed-use communities anchored by high-performing schools.

Derwin has spent the last decade in community development, public education, and venture capital with a particular focus on coalescing and maximizing community assets. Prior to Maslow, Derwin co-founded and served as the CEO of Gestalt Community Schools (GCS), a charter management organization that develops high-performing, community-based charter schools in Memphis, Tennessee. Under his leadership, GCS grew into one of the highest-performing networks of schools in Tennessee and anchored over forty acres of a mixed-use development that he spearheaded, including a performing arts center and affordable housing.

Derwin earned his BA in Psychology from Emory University, an MFA in Creative Writing from Hollins University, and a PhD in Educational Psychology from the University of Memphis. He has held board seats at arts, healthcare, foundation, and education-based companies. In 2015, Derwin became the youngest person to chair the board of Memphis Light, Gas and Water, the nation's largest three-tier public utility. In 2019, he joined the inaugural board of the governor-appointed Tennessee Public Charter School Commission. He is a Broad Academy Fellow and a member of the Aspen Global Leadership Network.

Dr. Elvira Souza Lima is a researcher trained in brain sciences, anthropology, music, psychology, and linguistics. She works in applied research in education, media, and culture and is the author of several books on literacy for all learners. She holds a doctorate from the Sorbonne (Paris, France), a postdoctoral degree in anthropology and linguistics from Stanford University (Palo Alto, California, USA) where she focused on how to reverse the school failure of Latina girls in fifth grade. She studied at the Collège de France Anthropologie with Claude Lèvi-Strauss and Neurobiologie de l'Enfant with Julian de Ajuriaguerra. She has additional degrees in music and piano. Follow her blog at http:// elvirasouzalima.blogspot.com

Pesquisadora com formação em ciências do cérebro, antropologia, música, psicologia e linguística. Fez doutorado na Sorbonne (Paris, França), pós doutoramento em antropologia e linguística na Stanford University (Palo Alto, California, EUA) centrado em como reverter o fracasso escolar de meninas latinas na quinta série. Estudou no Collège de France Antropologia com Claude Lèvi-Strauss e Neurobiologie de l'Enfant com Julian de Ajuriaguerra. É formada em música com especialização em piano.

Deanne Thomas is an experienced leader in indigenous education issues in New Zealand. She has developed a number of projects and programmes for teachers of Māori immersion, dual immersion and te reo Māori. She was a member of Te Ohu Matua, the reference group for the Ministry of Education in the development of Te Marautanga o Aotearoa. Deanne has been at the forefront of hangarau for Mā ori-medium schools. She has served on the Ministry of Education's Digital Technologies in the New Zealand Curriculum reference group. As Kaihautū Māori for CORE Education, Deanne works to grow the professional capability of the CORE Māori-medium facilitators and publishing teams. She also supports other Māori facilitators within CORE Education by providing a cultural base/network where people can celebrate and increase their personal understanding of te reo Mā ori, tikanga and mātauranga.

Across the company Deanne offers the advice and support required to help CORE meet its cultural aspirations as a company.

Saku Tuominen, co-founder and creative director of Idealist Group, is an entrepreneur, innovator, creative director, executive producer, author, keynote speaker, curator, olive oil producer, and right wing (in ice hockey). Idealist Group is a production company of ideas. The mission of the company is to improve the world with bold ideas that are executed well. At the moment Idealist Group concentrates on three main areas: the future of education, office work, and video.

Tom Vander Ark is an advocate for innovations in learning. As CEO of Getting Smart, he advises schools, districts, networks, foundations, and learning organizations on the path forward. A prolific writer and speaker, Tom is author of *Getting Smart; Smart Cities That Work for Everyone; Smart Parents; Better Together; The Power of Place;* and *Difference Making at the Heart of Learning.* He has published thousands of articles and co-authored more than fifty books and white papers. He writes regularly on GettingSmart.com, LinkedIn, and contributes to Forbes.

Previously he served as the first executive director of the Gates Education Initiative for the Bill & Melinda Gates Foundation. Tom served as a public-school superintendent in Washington State and has extensive private sector experience. Tom is a board member for Education Board Partners, Director for 4.0 Schools, Digital Learning Institute, Latinx Education Collaborative, Mastery Transcript Consortium and eduInnovation and an Advisor for One Stone and Teton Science Schools.

Dan Varner is the president and CEO at Goodwill Industries of Greater Detroit. Before joining Goodwill, Dan served as the CEO at Excellent Schools Detroit, a partnership of Detroit organizations working to improve Detroit's public education systems.

He has also worked as a program officer at the W.K. Kellogg Foundation on both the Michigan and Education & Learning teams. At the Foundation, he co-led the redevelopment of a local giving strategy for Detroit.

Dan is also the co-founder and former CEO of Think Detroit, a nationally recognized, award-winning youth development organization. Dan merged Think Detroit with Detroit PAL to create the largest provider of youth development sports programs in Detroit. The organization continues to operate as Detroit PAL today, and now serves 13,000 participants each year.

Dan has received many awards and his work has been recognized by two Presidential administrations. He serves on many boards of directors, including the ACLU of Michigan, ConnectEd, Capital Impact Partners, and Detroit PAL. He also served on Michigan's State Board of Education for four years. He is a current member of the Aspen Global Leadership Network. Dan is an attorney by training and is a graduate of the University of Michigan and the University of Michigan Law School.

Susanna Williams is program development and partnerships manager at Building Futures/Apprenticeship Rhode Island. Susanna is a lifelong educator and communications specialist with more than fifteen years of experience as a teacher, administrator, and strategic leader in K-12, higher education, and the philanthropic sector as well as political campaigns. Susanna led marketing, communications, and government relations at Renton Technical College, while also serving as the executive director of the Renton Technical College Foundation. She joined the Bill & Melinda Gates Foundation's Postsecondary Success team in 2012 after connecting with the director through a blind message on LinkedIn. Active on Twitter since 2009, Susanna is a strong advocate for the power of social media and the power of networks. A 2011 German Marshall Memorial Fellow, Susanna received her master's degree in Education from Bank Street College of Education and her undergraduate degree in Politics from Earlham College.

John J. Wood is the founder of Room to Read, a global nonprofit organization focused on literacy and gender equality in education. He is the author of *Creating Room to Read: A Story of Hope in the Battle for Global Literacy; Leaving Microsoft to Change the World: An Entrepreneur's Odyssey to Educate the World's Children;* and the children's book *Zak the Yak with Books on His Back.* He is a four-term member of the Clinton Global Initiative's Advisory Board and a Henry Crown Fellow at the Aspen Institute. John was selected for the inaugural class of Young Global Leaders by the World Economic Forum and was awarded Microsoft's first "Alumni of the Year" award by Bill and Melinda Gates. John has served on the Board of Directors for Net Impact and One Acre Fund and is currently an advisory board member of Global Citizen Year, New Story, and Possible Health.

Nicole Young is an educator, writer, coach, and founder of The Well Community Consulting. She previously served as executive director and head of school at Bard Early College in New Orleans after working at the United States Department of Education and the White House in the Obama administration. Nicole graduated from the University of South Carolina with a bachelor's degree in international studies, and from the University of Pennsylvania with an MSEd in education policy.

APPENDIX

In the introduction I shared a few options for how to interact with this book. The appendix is one of them. Just because a chapter title includes the word "language" for example, does not mean that it is the only chapter where interviews address issues of multilingualism in education. In the appendix you can track themes across all of the articles, so you may want to start there. Whichever path you choose, I encourage you to think about your own answer to the original "one good question." What experiences are you bringing to this question? What is it that you want to learn?